Money in
Your Mailbox

OTHER WILEY SMALL BUSINESS EDITIONS

Money in Your Mailbox

How to Start and Operate a Successful Mail-Order Business

Second Edition

L. PERRY WILBUR

WILEY

JOHN WILEY & SONS, INC.
New York · Chichester · Brisbane
Toronto · Singapore

Copyright © 1985, 1993 by L. Perry Wilbur
Published by John Wiley & Sons, Inc.

Library of Congress Cataloging-in-Publication Data
Wilbur, L. Perry.
   Money in your mailbox : how to start and operate a mail-order business / L. Perry Wilbur.
     p.   cm.
   Includes bibliographical references (p.   ) and index.
   ISBN 0-471-57775-8 (cloth : acid-free paper).—ISBN
0-471-57330-2 (paper : acid-free paper)
   1. Mail-order business—United States. 2. New business enterprises—United States. I. Title.
HF5466.W48   1993
658.8'72—dc20
                                    92-13550

Printed in the United States of America

10 9 8 7 6 5 4 3 2 1

Contents

PART III: MARKETING YOUR PRODUCT OR SERVICE

A Personal Note
to the Reader

W e live in truly remarkable times. The changing trends and incredible world events of the last few years have dwarfed the preceding half-century with their impact. It's as though a director is standing outside the arena of history saying, "You ain't seen nothing yet!" And it does make you wonder what is coming down the pike next.

So for the above reasons, a second edition of *Money in Your Mailbox* seemed in order, and I wish to thank my editor, Judith McCarthy, for the idea. I also want to thank the Wiley editorial, production, marketing, and rights teams for their continued support of the book.

In addition, my sincere thanks go to the readers who have bought and used the book. I have received many complimentary letters and phone calls from readers all over America, and from such distant places as London, Sydney, Australia, Hong Kong, and Canada.

In appreciation, I have sought to make this second edition even more valuable and helpful. Many new chapters and sections have been added. Today's mail-order operator will find helpful material on building a business, ways to beat the ever-increasing competition, more product-service suggestions, the latest direct mail ideas along with specific ways to upgrade direct mail profits, and additional advice on mailing lists.

The new section on marketing on a global basis should be especially helpful, along with products, services, and businesses in demand overseas, products that will sell in Europe and Japan, data-base marketing, and more specific guidelines on sure ways of making mail-order profits.

Other special bonus features include new directions on mail order as a part-time business, the best seasons for mail order, how to maximize year-round sales, and additional helpful resources in the appendix section. All this and much more should keep customer orders coming your way for years to come.

It is my sincere wish that this second edition of *Money in Your Mailbox* will prove to be a real treasure-trove of guidance, resources, information, and ideas that will lead you to new horizons of money-making profits and success. May this second edition lead you to a mail-order fortune and into an increasingly prosperous, successful twenty-first century. And may your mailbox stay crammed with orders year after year.

Preface to the First Edition

Ever wonder what it's like to find money in your mailbox day after day? Have you ever thought about starting a mail-order company through which you could launch a product or service and build a profitable business of your own—either part-time or full-time? If so, then this book is for you.

I started and operated a mail-order company of my own in preparation for writing this book, so much of the material is based on actual experience. I'll never forget the thrill of seeing the first cash orders in my mailbox. I know that by following the guidelines in this book you will be able to experience the same thrill.

In the following pages you'll discover that there's no business like the mail-order business. In mail order you're the boss. You can live anywhere you like and operate the business while holding down a regular job. You can start your business with limited funds and grow at whatever rate you think best.

All types of people can be found making good money in the mail-order business—single individuals, couples, families, students, retired people, moonlighters, working wives, or just about anyone who wants a profitable sideline. Many companies, both small and large, have set up mail-order divisions in order to capitalize on the money that can be made through the mail.

Mail order could open the doors of the good life for you. At the very least, the mail-order business is a proven way to a second income and a bank account that just keeps on growing. At the very best, the business can provide much more than a second income. The mail-order industry is famous for its millionaire success stories.

You may never make a million dollars running a mail-order company, but you can take in more money than you might expect—maybe more than you ever dreamed. You can become part of an amazing industry, one that has often been called the last frontier of fortune building.

I know there's a rewarding place for you in this exciting business. This book is meant to help you get started and to guide you in the operation of your company. Refer to it often as you build your business.

Welcome to the stimulating and unique world of mail order. May your profits be large and your mailbox overflow with cash orders.

L. PERRY WILBUR

Part I

GETTING STARTED IN MAIL ORDER

SUCCESS STORY: Bundle of Fun

Michele Lissie started a mail-order business based on the solid idea that too many toys children receive today don't require imagination. "Toys do everything for them. The market is flooded with high-tech toys." Examples of Michele's toys are puppets, books, and blocks. She offers no electronic or battery-operated toys.

"Creative toys that don't have a set function are the best," says Michele. A large cardboard box is a favorite among children. "They can cut it, paint it, or live in it."

1

A Mail-Order Business of Your Own

You in the mail-order business? Why not? There are numerous reasons why you should at least consider the idea. A mail-order business can provide either an ideal leisure-time activity or an excellent business opportunity. A mail-order business offers a high profit potential and can generate a very substantial additional income. Many mail-order businesses take only a few hours a day to run. A lot of firms in business today are owned and operated by one person working alone. You'd be surprised how prosperous most of the established firms are.

Look at the facts. The *Wall Street Journal* estimates the total annual revenue from mail order at between $55 and $65 billion. That's a lot of money winging its way through the mails in this country. Why can't you get in on some of the action? Do people really buy this much by mail? You'd better believe they do, and they are going to be buying even more in the years to come.

Can anyone get into mail order? Yes. Just about anyone can get into the business. Of course, your chances for real success and big profits are much better if you have a few of the qualities that are most helpful in the business. In the words of the Department of Commerce, "In mail-order work, anyone with imagination, determination, and a willingness to study and experiment may have very little difficulty getting started. A number of the most successful one-man operations obtain an income as high as $40,000 to $100,000 a year." Many part-time firms take in from $15,000 to $40,000.

Total mail-order business is expected to double in size in the next decade. Why the big boom? Well, one reason is that more people are moving from the cities to the suburbs. Many Americans are getting fed up with the lack of service characteristic of so many stores today. Millions of buyers are, therefore, sending in their orders by mail. Shopping by mail saves them time, trouble, and usually money.

Another more or less psychological reason why people do business by mail is that they enjoy anticipating the arrival of their purchases. It gives them a pleasant feeling to know their order is on the way. Perhaps even a sense of mystery is involved.

WHAT TO SELL BY MAIL

Okay. Granted there's a prosperous future ahead, at least for the wise mail-order dealers who choose the right products and services to offer. But how does a newcomer like yourself decide what to sell by mail?

The best answer to this key question is to be a copycat. That's right. In the mail-order business it's far wiser to offer a product that's already being sold successfully through the mail. Address labels, printing services, books, correspondence courses, information, health foods, religious materials, clothing, foot-care materials, and many other product categories are all time-tested and being sold successfully by mail today. It's best to avoid starting a new and untested product or service until you learn more about the business and gain some helpful experience. You can always originate new products later, after you have learned how to test them and have mastered the fine points of launching a new product. In the beginning it's best to stick with proven sellers. See Chapter 5 on choosing your product or service.

Some of the best ideas for products can be picked up by browsing through the pages of some leading mail-order publications. Just a few of the many products advertised recently included a music scroll, a portable dishwasher, an exerciser, a family tree book and chart, a dog bed, an oxygen inhaler, a coat of arms emblem, a personalized rubber stamp, a vast assortment of how-to-do-it books, a secret money belt, rapid reading records, and reading glasses. All of these products are evidently selling. If they weren't, you can bet that these mail-order companies would discontinue them.

What do most of these successful mail-order products have in common? The first thing you notice is that they're all unusual. Most of the offerings have unique or otherwise attractive features. Many are items or products that you can't buy just anywhere. Many mail-order products are sold exclusively through the mail. If customers want the particular product advertised, they may have no choice but to purchase it from the company selling it by mail—a most enviable situation for the dealer.

Other attractions of successful mail-order products include price advantage, personalization, and, especially with novelty products, uniqueness. The key to success in mail order is, of course, the product. Select a product that people need or want, and you're halfway home to good profits.

There are two basic ways to obtain the products you sell by mail. One very popular arrangement is to have various suppliers drop-ship to your customers. In most drop-shipping arrangements you send your customer's order to your supplier, along with a shipping label addressed to your customer under your own company name. Your supplier then fills the order using your shipping label. This way you avoid having to keep a stock of the product on hand. The companies that drop-ship for you offer a special drop-ship price to you as their dealer. The difference between the retail price and the special drop-ship price is where you make your profit. Basically, you are supplying the customer order and the drop-ship company is supplying the product for you.

The second method is to keep the product on hand yourself. The problems with this method usually come from the need to calculate in advance how much stock to keep. You can't be sure how many orders you might receive. Either too much stock or too little can create problems. If possible, it's a good idea to try out both methods in a limited way until you decide which you like best.

WAYS TO GET MAIL-ORDER CUSTOMERS

How does a mail-order business owner get customers? There are a number of ways, but, if you decide to try mail order part-time, the best way is to get your first orders by advertising. Does this mean that you have to understand advertising and place your own ads? Well, you do need to know the basics, but these can be mastered quickly. You'll need to know what goes into a pulling ad, how to write one, and the best times to run one. Of course, these all depend on what you're selling.

Nine out of ten new mail-order operators start the same way. They pick a good product and then work up what they feel will be an effective classified ad. Next, they test their ad by running it in a few proven mail-order publications. If the ad pulls in enough orders to make a profit, they run the same ad in additional mail-order publications. There are other ways to get orders, but the classified ad route is the best way to start (see Chapters 8 and 9). If you like the mail-order business and decide to stick with it you might eventually experiment with other ways to get orders, such as display ads and direct mail. Until you have a lot of mail-order experience under your belt, you should stay with small and inexpensive classified ads. Even these small ads are getting more expensive, as rate-per-word continues to climb. Test your ads first, to be sure you have a winner. Run your ads in proven mail-order publications like *Specialty Salesman, Popular Mechanics, Popular Science,* or *Mechanix Illustrated.* If you receive enough orders to recover the cost of your ad, the cost of the product itself, and any costs of shipping and handling, then you'll want to advertise in an increasing number of mail-order publications. If you have a good product, this is the way your business will grow.

Advertising is not the only way to handle mail order. Direct mail is growing rapidly as a very profitable wing of the mail-order industry. Today 37 percent of what's in the average mailbox is an unsolicited sales pitch. That's 18 pieces of mail per person, per month. More about direct mail later in the book.

If you are planning to rely on advertising, keep in mind that it's easier to sell lower-priced items through your ads. Selling a $10.00 product directly from an ad takes more words than are usually available in the average classified ad. Today the cost per word in many of the leading mail-order publications varies from $7.00 to $15.00 or more per word. The higher-priced items require a bigger and more expensive selling job. A product or service that sells for about $5.00 to $10.00 is usually best when you're first starting out.

START SMALL AND GROW SLOWLY

Mail order offers you all kinds of possibilities, once you've learned the basics. I have run my own mail-order business on a part-time basis for many years. I offer several instructional products and also low-priced booklets. It cost me about $100.00 to get started, but I started in a small way and have been content to grow slowly. My greatest expenses have been advertising and printing costs.

I strongly advise you to start your mail-order business as a sideline. There's no need to jump into the business full-time, hoping to get rich quickly. Before you go full-time there is a lot you should learn, and this will take some time. You can learn the basics in a few weeks or months. The ideal way to begin is to start small and grow slowly, while continuing to learn as much as you possibly can about the business.

CHOOSING YOUR COMPANY NAME

One of the first things you should do when setting up your own mail-order business is to decide on a company name. Then have some professional-looking letterheads and business envelopes printed showing the company name and address. Black on white, or one or two colors, is fine for the printing.

It's best to use a simple name for your company, and it's usually a good idea to use your own name for the company. Why? By using your own name, you won't have to get a special city, state, or county license to operate your mail-order business. It's perfectly alright to use your own name and add "company" after it (for example, The Bill Jones Company or The Joan Stevens Company). Don't use "Inc." after your name. You're not allowed to do this unless you have actually formed a legal corporation. When I started my own business, I simply used the word "enterprises" after my own last name. So my company's name was Wilbur Enterprises. It still is today. In recent years, many mail-order companies have used "enterprises," so I recommend you come up with a more original word. Some examples are Sanders and Sons, Simplicity Toys, Custom Prints, and Amazing Products. We're getting close to the turn of a new century, so perhaps you could use Twenty-First Century Company as a name. That's four words, but it sounds fresh and new. An advantage in using a short name (two words, if possible) is the money it will save in running ads.

Many mail-order firms use a box number for their address, but it's better and more businesslike to use an actual street address. Remember: Those who see your ads and buy your products will be sending you checks and money orders, and to them it will seem much safer and more reliable to have a street address rather than a box number. Some people are just naturally suspicious and skeptical, so always make it easy for a buyer to do business with you. This is one of the signposts to success in mail order. (By the way, I suggest you discourage customers from sending cash through the mail as a rule, although you may lose some orders.)

WHAT YOU NEED TO GET STARTED

Many mail-order firms have been started with $100.00 or less. The amount of money you need depends on the type of product or service you're offering. Once you've decided on a company name, you will need letterheads imprinted with your company name, mailing address labels, regular and business return envelopes, pens, paper, and a record book to keep track of orders received and filled. A typewriter or word processor is a virtual necessity, since your business letters should be typed on your letterheads. You can rent one of these machines if you don't own one.

FINDING AND USING A PRINTER

A reliable and skilled printer you can trust and depend on is a must in mail order. You can easily see why you need the services of a professional printer from the start—it's virtually impossible to launch your mail-order business without professional-looking letterheads. You'll be sending out a lot of business letters, so letterheads are a primary need.

Wherever you live, there's probably at least one quality printer in the area. Most large cities have a number of printers. You should take the time to visit a few in person. Introduce yourself. Ask the printer for some samples of work and look them over carefully. Tell the printer that you may soon have some printing orders and that you're considering several different printers for the job. Request a price list for various kinds of printing, including letterheads, reply envelopes, order cards and forms, circulars, and any other materials you use regularly in your business. Be sure to ask about any savings on quantity printing orders. The more copies of an item you have printed, the cheaper the price usually is. Printers often offer special discounts on various printing orders, so it's helpful to be on their mailing lists.

You'll have a lot of printing orders while running your mail-order business, so a printer that does quality work is a four-star plus in your favor. As your business grows and develops, you'll have an even greater need for a good printing service. The following are ways to find good printers:

1.   Scan the local newspapers and magazines in your area for the names of various printers. Then go and check them out. Ask for samples of their work.

2. Look under "printing" in the advertising sections of leading mail-order publications. Then write to the listed companies, asking for brochures and details on their printing services and rates.
3. Contact established mail-order companies and ask them to recommend a quality printer.
4. Look for printing service ads in magazines and newspapers like *The Writer, Writer's Digest,* and the *Wall Street Journal.*
5. Ask a respected advertising agency in your area to recommend a printer who has done quality work for them.
6. Look up some printing firms in the Yellow Pages. Visit several before deciding which one is the best.

Mail-Order Printers

If you can't locate a quality printer in your area, or you're just not pleased with the choice of available printers, try writing to a printer in some other city or area. The mail-order industry is served by a number of quality mail-order printers. You'll see their ads by looking through mail-order publications like *Popular Science, House Beautiful, Mechanix Illustrated,* and the *Wall Street Journal.* A shipping charge will, of course, be added to any printing orders sent by mail. Extra time must also be allowed for your orders to be received, filled, and shipped back to you. Orders for letterheads, circulars without photos, reply envelopes, and most order forms don't take too long as a rule. But four-page sales letters or 50-page booklets can take weeks or even months to be printed and shipped. Some printers work faster than others, but the printing quality may suffer.

Ordering from Printers

In my own experience with printers, I find that many of them seem to be extra busy at certain times of the year. Most of the better printers are swamped with work during holiday periods.

Whenever you have a fairly large or important printing order, it's a good idea to contact your printer in advance with a projected date. This advance notice isn't necessary for small orders.

Some mail-order operators phone their big orders in to the printer. When printers are told to be ready for upcoming orders, it can be a great help and time-saver for both you and your printer. Printers like to plan their work schedule ahead, so they can get orders out as quickly and efficiently as possible.

You don't have to understand a lot of technical printing terms in order to obtain quality work. It does help, however, if you can talk to your printer in person. You can then explain just what you want done on any special orders.

Offset Printing

Most of the printing done in mail order today is *offset*. As a mail-order operator, you take or send your material (to be printed) to a printer in camera-ready form. This means that whatever you wish to be printed must be ready to be photographed by your printer. After the photograph has been taken, an offset plate is made from the photo negative. Your printer can then turn out any number of copies you want.

Your sales letters, circulars, and order forms can be printed by offset, but it's usually better to have your business letterheads done by *letterpress* (a form of printing using actual type).

Special Printing Orders

You may occasionally have a special form, insert, circular, or flatsheet (a single sheet of copy you want duplicated) to be printed. Ask your printer how quickly such orders can be filled, for there will be times when you suddenly realize that you need copies of a new form or a special circular.

Check over your supplies regularly to avoid running out of reply envelopes, sales letters, order forms, or circulars when you need them most. Be sure to submit refill orders long before your present supply is exhausted.

Payment for Printing Orders

Practically all printers expect payment in full with each printing order you send them. On the other hand, if you stick with one printing firm and give it a large amount of business over a period of time, it's quite possible that the firm will grant you credit and allow you to make a downpayment on your printing order with the balance due when it is filled and shipped to you.

It's also true that you can get to know a printer on a personal basis. In time, you might come to trust each other so that a credit arrangement could be worked out. Many printers now accept credit cards for payments.

More Tips on Printers

One good way to insure that you always have access to quality printers is to use an out-of-town printer as a backup. This way you can be virtually certain that you can get action on your printing orders regardless of circumstances.

Something else to remember about printers is that they're generally competitive. One printer may do your order for you for less money than another. It will pay to shop around and compare prices before you decide to give your business to any one printer. For example, a mail-order printer may do the work cheaper and just as effectively as a local company.

One benefit of contacting a number of printers is that many of them will put your name on their mailing lists. This means that you'll be sure to hear about special orders, co-op printing deals, price-cuts, copy preparation information, and the like. Printers may also obtain your name and address from the printing firm you deal with and put you on their own mailing lists. This is a good way for you to find new printers.

SOURCES OF ADDITIONAL HELP

Before you launch your company, you might wish to contact the following sources for additional help and guidance. Ask them to send you their free folders and pamphlets on mail order. There may be a small charge for certain folders, but most are free. Request them soon, in case their supplies are limited. These folders may not be available later, and the current addresses might also be subject to change. Here are the addresses:

- Small Business Administration Ask for the pamphlet on "Selling
  1441 L Street, N.W. by Mail Order."
  Washington, D.C. 20416

- Superintendent of Documents Request a copy of "Guides
  U.S. Government Against Deceptive Ads."
  Printing Office
  Washington, D.C. 20402

- Council of Better
  Business Bureaus
  1515 Wilson Boulevard
  Washington, D.C. 20036

  Ask for their free folder, "Tips on Mail-Order Profit Mirages." You might also request the pamphlet entitled "Code of Advertising." There may be a small charge for it.

- Income Opportunities Magazine
  380 Lexington Avenue
  New York, NY 10017

  Offers various pamphlets and information on mail order for usually small amounts.

My other book, *How to Make Money in Mail Order,* John Wiley & Sons, $14.95, may also be helpful to you. It is for the more advanced mail-order businessperson.

If you like the sound of this business and can see yourself in it part-time, by all means read more about it. Your library will have a number of good books on the business, and several known mail-order publications offer inexpensive booklets on how to actually start your own company. *House Beautiful* is one of these. The Small Business Administration can also send you information. It's a good idea to write to these sources and request information.

The best way to really learn the business, however, is to actually get into it. Send your order to a printer for professional letterheads, along with regular business and return envelopes. Then you can start communicating in a businesslike way. You can grow from that point forward, as you build a profitable mail-order company of your own.

SUCCESS STORY: Entrepreneur Chalks Up $700,000 in Sales Last Year of Hangover Helper, Morning-After Pain Pills

This clever inventor is Eric Summers of Jacksonville Beach, Florida. He started his business as a joke in 1981 but is now a fast-growing, big success story.

2

The Self-Employment Picture

MAIL ORDER IS SELF-EMPLOYMENT

Once you get your mail-order business launched, you will have joined the ranks of the self-employed. To be honest about it, there are two sides to the self-employment picture. There are both advantages and disadvantages to working for yourself. You need to be aware of both sides of the coin.

You'll have plenty of company on the day you start your mail-order business. The Small Business Administration says that 1,000 new businesses are started every day in the United States alone. Fifty percent fail in the first two years. Eighty-five percent fail in the first five years. Not all of these new businesses are mail-order companies; but still, the number of new businesses of all types that fail is shockingly large.

WHY NEW BUSINESSES FAIL

The SBA says that there's one chance in five that a new business will still be operating under the original owner after a 10-year period. According to the SBA 92.1 percent of new businesses fail because of lack of management ability, 1.1 percent because of neglect, three-fifths of 1 percent for fraud, .6 percent because of disaster, and the remaining 5.6 percent for unknown reasons.

THE GOOD SIDE OF SELF-EMPLOYMENT

When you have considered both the pros and cons of self-employment you may well find that the advantages of being your own boss far outweigh the disadvantages. A great many people are much happier running their own businesses. The idea of being their own boss is tremendously appealing to millions of people. You come and go as you please. You control the pace of your work. And there's a big challenge in running things yourself. People who work for themselves usually have more incentive to do well, to succeed, for they are, in effect, gambling that they can make it.

A Ready-Made Career

Should you decide to join the ranks of the self-employed, you'll have solved one increasingly difficult problem automatically. Actually, you will have bypassed the problem by creating your own job. You won't have to get involved in a tedious and possibly futile search for a rewarding job.

In a recent year, over 300,000 new teachers left college with bachelor's or master's degrees. The National Educational Association reported that over 100,000 of these qualified new teachers were unable to find teaching positions. Go to work for yourself, and you'll never have to worry about waking up to find that you're out of a job. In self-employment, you're the top dog.

Self-Employment Develops Your Energies and Abilities

Working for yourself calls into play your individual energies and abilities. Today, millions of workers the world over complain of being employed in meaningless, uninteresting work. Holding down such a job, year after year, may permanently stifle ambition and drive.

Why spend five or 10 years in a job you could grow to hate, when you have a chance to launch your own business and do your own thing? Instead of having to drag yourself to work in the morning, the challenging work involved with your own company would probably make you eager to get to work.

In the words of Cecil Humphreys, former president of Memphis State University, "This generation of college students is very much aware that society is changing rapidly, and they are expecting from their college experiences something that will better equip them to not only live in, but contribute more to a rapidly changing society."

Who knows? You might well be able to contribute much more to society as a self-employed worker and owner-operator of your own mail-order business. Working for yourself might even prove to be less of a gamble than casting your lot with an employer.

You Can't Be Fired

That brings us to another great advantage of self-employment: You can't be fired. Newspapers and magazines frequently carry stories about companies that have let longtime employees go in order to save money or trim their staffs. Often these workers have given 20 years or more of their lives to the company. If and when you decide to go to work for yourself, you won't have to live with a fear that haunts millions—the fear of losing your job. Such a disaster can never happen when you're the boss—unless, of course, you fire yourself.

The Attraction of Money

Another lure of self-employment is money. Running your own business eliminates the ceiling on your potential earnings. This is especially true in mail order. It's still very possible to make a fortune in a business of your own.

Many self-employed people see their annual incomes rise year after year. It takes hard work, of course, but the point is that nobody can step in and say you can't make any more money. Your salary can't be frozen, and nobody can beat you out of a promotion, because you're the boss. It's your company; it's your business.

Being Happy in Your Work

A major consideration that you shouldn't overlook is job contentment. Would you be happier working for yourself rather than for someone else? Karl Menninger has stated that three-fourths of psychiatric patients suffer from dissatisfaction in their work.

Another serious question related to job contentment is the question of personal progress. Ask yourself what type of work you can advance in most quickly—working for a company or for yourself? Bear in mind that although self-employment may be tough going until you are established, it's very possible to reap a rich harvest, eventually making far more than you could ever earn with an employer.

Let's face it. The name of the game today is progress. Everybody wants to move up the success ladder. Your work years will go by fast. If you don't move up, or if you get stuck somewhere in the climb, you may not have long to enjoy the so-called good life.

How about the chance to see the direct results of your own efforts? This possibility alone draws many into self-employment. The results of your planning and effort are especially apparent in mail order. Come up with an attractive product or service, and you will quickly see results. Your level of success will be directly related to your overall planning and advertising strategy.

SOME DISADVANTAGES OF SELF-EMPLOYMENT

Can You Make Decisions?

To understand both sides of the picture, you need to be aware of some aspects of self-employment that might trip you up. One possible pitfall is the decision-making process itself.

Can you make decisions? Is it easy or agonizing for you to make important decisions? Do you put off making decisions whenever possible? You must answer these questions honestly when you consider launching your own business. Once you get into business, nobody will be there to make the many needed decisions for you. The way you handle decisions will determine whether you sink or swim. If you find it difficult to make sound decisions, you should probably forget about starting your own business.

The right decisions are vital to the growth of a new business. Make the wrong decisions, and you alone are the villain. Still, keep in mind that you can't determine the overall quality of your judgment until you begin to use it and actually start making business decisions.

The Risk of Going into Debt

Another worrisome aspect of self-employment is the inescapable fact that most self-employed people are forced to go into debt. It may take some time to become established in mail order or any other new business.

During this period you will have to make some sacrifices in the area of financial security. Millions find it tough to give up the peace of mind that security assures you. You won't be sure about your life-style until you've become established.

On the other hand, a great many who launch a mail-order business do so on a part-time basis. It's possible to hold down a regular job and still run a mail-order company. I've done it myself. Running a mail-order company can take anywhere from a few hours a day up to 40 or more hours a week. It all depends on the size and scope of your business. The time involved will also depend on how slowly or quickly you wish to grow. You will almost certainly start small and grow slowly. So you could be in mail order with a commitment of only a few hours a day.

Good Health Is a Must

Generally speaking, good health is important for success in self-employment. You could be financially wiped out, should you lose your health while self-employed. As the boss, if you miss a few days or weeks, you can get behind quickly and go down the drain. Handicapped people, however, have managed to run mail-order companies and have turned a handsome profit doing it. It depends on the person's total abilities.

Keeping Up with Changes in Your Field

When you're not actually on the job, running your business, much of your free time will be spent keeping up with the changing state of the business. There's a real need to stay well informed on all changing developments in postal rates and laws, product information, taxes, and various other aspects of the mail-order business. You'll want to know, too, what other products and services are being offered and how well they seem to be doing. This means devoting time to research.

An Extra Work Day Each Week

One fact that discourages millions of people is that self-employed workers spend more time on the job (one extra day each week, according to a government study) than those who are not self-employed. With many workers looking forward to the four-day work week, this extra day of work appears to be too big a sacrifice. But, as already pointed out, a mail-order business need not take this much time at all, at least not until it has grown by leaps and bounds. At that point, you'll probably be making enough money so that you'll be able to hire others to handle the extra workload. Besides, when you're working on a winner you probably won't mind putting in a little extra time yourself.

Perhaps it is because success as a self-employed person requires a healthy amount of hard work, good luck, sound judgment, and persistence that only one-tenth of all who work for a living actually work for themselves. Many try self-employment for a time, but find that they lack the skills or abilities needed in the business they selected. So they go back to working for somebody else.

HOW MANY PEOPLE ARE SELF-EMPLOYED?

Of the seven million self-employed people in the United States, half are professionals—doctors, lawyers, dentists, and the like. One-fourth of the self-employed are independent farmers. The rest of the seven million operate small businesses such as motels, groceries, gas stations, retail establishments, museums, and various consumer-type stores. Many people are self-employed because they have few other choices. Many have no clearly defined skills that can be marketed profitably to a prospective employer.

CONCLUSIONS ABOUT SELF-EMPLOYMENT

Even though success cannot be assured, millions of people the world over work for themselves and wouldn't have it any other way. Wherever one lives, there's something inviting and highly stimulating about waking up each morning knowing that you're in charge of yourself and your work. That's freedom! And it's most satisfying.

Part of the joy of working for yourself, aside from the unlimited possibilities, is the knowledge that you're in control of your work, and, to a large extent, your destiny. As a mail-order operator and self-employed writer, I can vouch for this truth.

Since joining the ranks of free-lance writers and launching my own mail-order business, I've come alive as never before. I'm anxious to start work each morning. The reason is that I like my work. It is work that interests me tremendously. I choose the products and services I will offer and the publications in which I will run my ads. I select the publications I will write for and the subjects I will write about. I work at my own pace and can usually work on my writing assignments anywhere I like. I also get to travel, gathering material and doing interviews.

A few years ago, Sheryl Bodily, of Columbia Falls, Montana, decided to leave the security of a steady job and try his luck as a self-employed professional artist. He had worked full-time at a local sawmill for 10 years while painting part-time. He decided that he was good enough to support his wife and six children by the sale of his artwork alone. He proved he was right.

Bodily's paintings—most of which depict western scenes or the activities of Indians—are now widely acclaimed. His first exhibit was in Hungry Horse, Montana. Since then, other work from his brush has been displayed throughout the United States.

Today there's an eager market for Bodily's work, because he believed that he could make it in self-employment and took the plunge. By taking the plunge and launching your own mail-order company, you may well be taking the most important career step of your life. Think well on it.

In summary, before you decide to join the ranks of the self-employed, be sure to consider the following points:

1. Most new businesses fail because of a lack of business knowledge and ability. Make it a point to find out as much as you possibly can about all aspects of your new business. Take careful stock of your abilities before you make your decision.

2. Ask yourself if you would be happier working for yourself. There are many advantages, but you must realize that there are plenty of headaches and problems to contend with as well. You will be the boss. Will you be happy being the person in charge?

3. Do you have enough discipline to succeed in self-employment? Remind yourself that nobody will be looking over your shoulder or motivating you to succeed. It's completely up to you. Do you have what it takes to motivate yourself month after month? A high degree of motivation is required to run a mail-order operation.

4. Can you work effectively alone? Many people prefer to work with others or for a large company. Certain types of self-employment require one to work alone much of the time. Mail order does, for the most part. Could you handle it?

5. Are you willing to work extra hard during the first years, in order to establish yourself? Starting your own company will require it.

6. Are you good at making decisions? If you dislike making deci-
    sions, it might be a mistake for you to go into self-employment.
    The right decisions at the right time are absolutely vital to the
    success of any self-employment venture, including mail order.
    You should keep in mind that the ability to make decisions can be
    developed. You might do better at it than you think.

7. Is your health good enough to hold up in the self-employment
    field? Ask yourself if you could keep up the pace needed, with-
    out your health suffering. At first, you might run your business
    for only a few hours each day. But later, with more customers
    and an increasing number of orders, you might need eight hours
    a day or more. In most cases, however, you can control the size
    of your business.

There you have it. Self-employment is certainly not for everyone. But
for those who can responsibly handle this kind of freedom—and enjoy
it—it's the only way to work and be happy. Many who were newcomers
to mail order several years ago wouldn't consider doing anything else
today. Many a thriving business would never have gotten off the ground if
those involved hadn't decided to become their own bosses.

In the final analysis, there's only one way to find out if self-
employment, and mail order in particular, is the work for you. Try it and
see if you like it. Go into it in a small way and see what happens. Chances
are that once you begin to make money in mail order, you'll want to get
into the business full-time. Seeing cash orders in your mailbox day after
day can spoil you for other kinds of work. But don't give up the position
you now hold on the hope of making a fast killing in mail order. Some do
earn good profits for their first months in the business, but there's no
guarantee. Try to resist a full-time involvement in the industry until you
know you're ready for it.

MAIL ORDER: THE PERFECT
PART-TIME BUSINESS

The majority of those who start their own mail-order companies begin on
a part-time basis. It makes good sense to proceed slowly in any new
venture that requires risk. As in any other business, there is risk involved
in running a mail-order firm. It's possible to choose the wrong product at
first. Many newcomers don't have the funds to do much advertising. And

it usually takes some time to develop the basic skills needed to sell products and services by mail.

Mail order is so exciting that you may soon find it hard to spend just a few hours each day or week on your new company. Working for yourself may generate such great enthusiasm that you may start wishing you could work around the clock. Reading and hearing about various success stories in the industry can also keep you eager to get moving toward the real profits to be made from selling by mail. But your chances of doing well later will be considerably strengthened if you can be content with being a part-timer for a while. Mail order is a wonderful part-time business. Some even call it the perfect part-time business. Here are just a few of the many reasons why this is so:

1. Starting part-time requires a smaller amount of money than starting full-time.

2. If your first product or offer proves to be a dud, you don't go down the drain. You haven't risked everything on your business.

3. You have the time to test new offers or products. You're not under the pressure of having to be certain that you'll make a good profit.

4. You can operate your company during your spare time. It's convenient and will fit in with almost any job.

5. You have time to think about product choice and to look over those items that are currently being sold successfully.

6. A part-time business requires less storage space for supplies.

7. Since you run fewer ads as a part-timer, you'll have the time to experiment with good ads using effective selling copy.

8. You can chart your future mail-order goals without worry. After all, you have another job.

9. Your printing and other business expenses can be kept to a minimum.

10. You'll find it refreshing and stimulating to turn from your regular daily work to the operation of your mail-order company.

11. You can grow at your own rate and thereby increase your chances for lasting success. The choice is always yours—whether to stay small or expand into a large company.

12. There's no limit to the profits you can earn in mail order.

Working on a part-time basis will stimulate your plans for the future and provide the knowledge and experience you will need if you decide to go after the really big money later.

See pages 6–7, 30 for more information on mail order as a part-time business. Few other businesses or sideline operations offer as much opportunity and profit potential as a mail-order company of your own. Remember: Fortune favors the bold. Your decision to enter mail order might just change your life.

3

20 Ways to Beat
the Competition

Here are 20 key tips on beating your competition.

1. **Produce a superior product.** America used to be unquestionably second to none, but in today's fast-paced global market some say we are slipping from first place. A number of world and business leaders have been calling America a second-rate producer.

In your own business, one of the most specific ways to rise above your competition is to go back to the drawing board and come up with a four-star product or service that does the job better, has clearly superior quality, works faster, cleaner, and more economically, and so on down the list.

2. **Let the market for your product know about it. Advertise.** You might have one of the best mail-order products in the world, but if you don't make your market aware of it, your competition will run over you like a steamroller. You must advertise your product, and do so both effectively and consistently.

Have you ever noticed how some ads in magazines, and most commercials on television, repeat themselves? Some of the auto advertisers and a nationally known popcorn brand often run their commercials back-to-back.

An advertising campaign requires a series of well-planned ads run in the right places over a designated period of time. I still remember the key ad phrase used for many years for Quaker Puffed Wheat cereal: "Shot from guns." You couldn't help but remember it and the cereal.

Getting products and services to register in the minds and memories of prospective customers is serious business. If you don't advertise effectively, and often enough, you do so at the peril of your product-service.

3. **Focus on the important priorities in running your business more efficiently.** Such priorities might include delegating important tasks to assistants, streamlining your operation, upgrading productivity, and handling employee conflicts. In the long run, a more efficient company can and usually will beat the competition offered by a disorganized, poorly managed company.

4. **Having knowledge of the competition you face is a great help in rising above it.** In the words of one business leader in Florida, "such knowledge includes knowing where your company can effectively compete and where it should not compete. For example, one shouldn't try to make cars like General Motors because they'll beat you every time."

A two-year study conducted by 16 faculty members of the Massachusetts Institute of Technology produced a several hundred-page report on what is wrong with American corporations (mostly the big ones). Some of the major factors hurting U.S. companies are "outdated corporate strategies." Foreign companies build high-quality goods, while many American corporations are still "mass producing like Henry Ford."

More knowledge across the board is an absolute must, for both small and large businesses, in winning against the competition. According to *Elks* magazine, "930 out of every 1000 businesses fail due to lack of business knowledge and ability." Obviously, if your competition has more useful knowledge, and applies it consistently better than you do, they'll be hard to beat. So obtaining knowledge and putting it into action yourself, on a regular basis, can do much to keep you head and shoulders above your competition.

5. **Small firms that diversify often run the risk of losing the focus that created their success.** Some businesspeople believe that placing all your eggs in one basket, giving all your focus to one product, sooner or later gets you into trouble. Others disagree and say that diversifying is dangerous.

One well-established product can of course be an important foundation in the early stages of your business. Gregory Fischbach launched a video game company, and it became a big success. His company took off fast. But in the words of Fischbach, "Being a one-product company, no matter what the category is, places the company in a vulnerable position."

According to Frank Hoy, professor of family-owned business at Georgia State University, "It's typical to have all your eggs in one basket. To diversify runs the risk of losing focus. A lot of companies run into terrible problems by jumping off into other areas, away from where their expertise is."

Not jumping off into other areas, when your competition does, could well result in victory—assuming their risk turns into disaster, which might very well happen. At least while you're starting, stick with what you know best.

6. **Develop and cultivate new or existing customers with special savings, premiums, or bonuses.** This method has increased sales and profits for lots of companies that do part of their business, or all of it, by mail order. If customers don't buy your mainline item, they may well go for one of the additional offers they find in your mailing package. Just be careful not to charge *too* little; you don't want to lose your profit.

7. **If your company receives orders via the mail, include additional offers in your mailing package.** Someone who has already ordered from you once is a great potential customer for more. This is a key way to get reorders without paying for ads or additional postage.

8. **Send out advance notice of special sales or discounts your company plans to offer.** This is a proven way to build customer goodwill. And if your competition fails to do it, it will place your company in the forefront of your customer's mind.

9. **Seek out new markets your company can capitalize on.** Avia International, a division of footwear maker Reebok International, estimated there may be as many as 500,000 mall walkers in the United States. This was a vast new market for Avia, and they went for it by introducing a $45 walking shoe designed to give extra traction.

10. **Consider reintroducing a fading product or service item.** There may still be a lot of steam (and sales) left in an old product you thought was dead. This may be a gamble, but it can pay off if you're right. By way of example, Hasbro, a toy company, acquired the Cabbage Patch Kids and believes there are a lot of sales left in these cuddly dolls.

11. **If they're well-planned and go over in a positive way, publicity stunts can reap a goldmine of profits for your company.** Joseph E. Levine, the late film producer, once staged a very successful publicity stunt, which was his first. Levine "rented" $1 million from a bank to display at a luncheon in New York to promote the British film *Jack the Ripper*. In Levine's own words, "I actually held up the cash . . . and thumped it on the table in front of me. I said, 'You know what this is, it's a million dollars, and the next time you see it, it will be working for you.' "

Levine was also credited with inventing "saturation booking," the practice of releasing a film across the country with tremendous promotion.

12. **Know your customers.** This can be especially helpful to you if your business involves repeat orders. By knowing your customers, you tend to know after a while what they like. With this valuable information, you'll be better able to estimate how much business you will do. Much, of course, depends on what your product item or service happens to be.

13. **Be willing to gamble. Success and good fortune favor the bold. Your competition may not be willing to gamble.** Colonel Harlan Sanders, the distinguished founder of the Kentucky Fried Chicken chain, didn't even begin in the business until the age of 66. He certainly gambled that the years ahead in his new business would see the realization and successful growth of his idea and his special chicken recipes.

His gamble paid off beyond his dreams. Sanders is dead, but the business he launched and built into a huge success still follows his basic ideas and principles.

14. **Enlist a celebrity to sing the praises of your product or give an opinion of your company.** This may be easier said than done. If you can pull it off, it can definitely put you ahead of your competition. You don't have to use big-name people. Consider lesser known figures in your region or geographic area. Endorsements from well-known, prominent local people can often bring the results you want.

15. **Use more showmanship in your business.** Showmanship is the act of brightening up or making something attractive. It's not trickery or deceit. It's presenting something (like your business) in a compelling, appealing, and stimulating way. By using more showmanship in your business, you're bound to increase your profits and beat your competition. Appearance, conviction, vitality, a sense of the dramatic, and sincerity are all part of showmanship.

16. **Check to see if your company's products are right for the growing elderly market. Your competitors may be ignoring this group.** More and more products are being designed these days to fit the special needs of the booming elderly market. Many of these products and services are right for older customers, while also remaining popular with younger buyers. Such products include watches with large numbers, easy-to-load cameras, and a device that uses an electric motor to raise a mattress and box spring off the bed frame.

17. **Adapt yourself and your business to meet the changing times.** Giving your business an edge over your competition may well call

for adjustment and adaptation. People in business can best face today's challenges, problems, and demands by learning how to change with the times.

When the economy goes through good and bad cycles, this can call for adaptation. American companies and businesses wishing to do business in Europe in the 1990s and beyond will also have to adapt to the conditions of the new situation there. It's a brand new Europe today with even more changes on the way.

18. **Realize that today's customers and prospects expect and demand more value for their money.** The decade of the 1990s will be remembered as the era when buyers and customers sought more value for their money. Buyers in general have become more sophisticated. Being aware of this fact, and acting on it as you operate your business, can keep you ahead of your competition.

19. **Consider making changes in existing products.** The athletic shoe field is an example. Shoemakers like U.S. Shoe Corporation and Reebok International have introduced walking pumps that combine the comfort of sneakers with the stylishness of high-heels. Reebok believes that women won't mind paying a higher price for greater comfort and quality.

20. **See if you can carve a new market and increase sales by capitalizing on changing demographics.** The divorce rate, for example, is falling, while marriage is on the rise. How do the changing facts, and demographics, affect your business? Keeping up with these trends can guide you to the right actions in your business. And the happy result is that you soar over your competition.

There you have them. Twenty guidelines for beating your competition. Start applying these practical and useful pointers in your business, and you'll put your competition to shame.

4

Questions and Answers about Mail Order

PRELIMINARY CONSIDERATIONS

Q. *How much money can I make in mail order?*

A. Mail order is a billion-dollar industry and gives every sign of continuous growth in the future. How much money you can make depends on the quality of your products or services, the effectiveness and amount of your advertising, and the coordination of all elements of your mail-order business.

Q. *Is it possible to start a mail-order business without much knowledge of mail order?*

A. Yes. Many men and women—young and old—started with a basic desire to have their own business. But usually a good knowledge of mail order will save you time, money, and disappointment. It's still true that knowledge is power.

Q. *Do I need a lot of money to start a mail-order company?*

A. No. But with today's galloping inflation, the cost of everything is higher. Printing and advertising costs are up. Postage rates are rising. So many mail-order companies now start with $750.00 to $1,000.00. But others get started with as little as $500.00.

Q. *Can I operate a mail-order company secretly, without my family members or neighbors knowing about it?*

A. Possibly. Using a post office box number will give you some privacy. But many prospects are wary of sending orders to a box number. A street address is better, but not as private. You can use a code name, but someone at your address might wonder who's getting all the strange mail.

Q. *Can one idea for a mail-order product or service make me rich?*
A. Yes. It's certainly possible with the right idea. Look at the success story of Coca-Cola®. Though it's not a mail-order product, it's a good example of what one good idea can do for you. No one knew what to do with the initial batch of Coca-Cola®. Making candy from it was considered. Then someone came up with the right idea—bottle it. The rest is Coca-Cola® history.

Q. *If I can give my mail-order business only an hour or so of my time a day, will this hurt my chances for doing well?*
A. No. Most mail-order operators started on a part-time basis. Many operators have regular nine-to-five jobs and run their mail-order companies during their spare time. As long as you fill all orders promptly, there's usually no problem. But when your business begins to grow, you might need some help—or more time—to operate your business.

Q. *Is it more practical to stay out of mail order until I am able to devote full time to it?*
A. Not necessarily. I've found that running my mail-order business part-time gives me some variety in my work. Starting out in a growth field like mail order on a part-time basis could be the smartest move of your life.

Q. *Can you give me a simple formula for getting started in mail order?*
A. This five-point plan should get you started. It worked for me.

1. Make a list of products or services that are being sold successfully by mail—possible items for you to offer.
2. Try to think of a new product or service that you could produce yourself.
3. Narrow your list down to one or two items that suit your interests, funds, background, and energies.
4. Plan the copy for your first ad (either a classified ad or an inquiry and follow-up ad) and run it in a leading mail-order publication.
5. If results are good, place your advertising in other publications. If results are poor, try new copy. If results continue to be poor, scrap the product or service and start over.

Q. *Is the study of marketing in college helpful for someone interested in mail order?*

A. Yes. You won't get all the answers by a long shot because the best experience for mail order is on-the-job training—actually selling by mail. But a study of marketing will teach you basic business principles that are applicable to mail order. On the other hand, don't stay out of mail order just because you didn't study marketing and advertising in school. Theory in the classroom is one thing; selling a product by mail is something else.

Q. *What effect will the increasing number of working women have on the mail-order industry?*

A. It means more of a boom. With more women in the labor force, there will be more potential buyers for mail-order products and services. Women also have less time for shopping and are ordering by mail with increasing frequency.

Q. *How fast is mail order growing?*

A. Over a billion dollars a week are spent on mail-order products, representing 12 percent of all consumer purchases. And the years ahead look even better.

Q. *How many small businesses are there in the United States at present?*

A. The number is, of course, continually changing. But the total is currently running at over nine million.

Q. *How well have newcomers to mail order done with their first ads and products?*

A. A good example is John Sicher—he started in mail order by offering watches and calculators. He ran his first ad in thirty publications and his ad brought in an incredible 30,000 orders and a cash bonanza of over $600,000.

Q. *What are the most important elements for success in mail order?*

A. A good idea for a product or service and good judgment in advertising and selling that product or service.

CHOOSING A PRODUCT OR SERVICE

Q. *Are there any tips that might help me in coming up with a new product or service?*

A. A good idea for one person might be a poor idea for someone else, but here is a tip that could easily guide you to one or more fine product or service items: There's a huge new interest in marriage. So you might try to dream up, plan, and produce a product or service that would appeal to married couples. There will be millions of new marriages, and these new families will need and want all sorts of things. I'm working on this myself and am convinced that it will pay off handsomely.

Q. *Before investing time, money, and effort in producing a product for mail order, is there a way to judge the quality of what the competition is offering?*

A. Looking at ads in leading mail-order publications will quickly tell you what's being offered. But you should do more than this. Order some mail-order products and look them over. If, for example, you're thinking of offering an informational booklet, you should send for similar booklets being sold and look them over carefully. See how they compare with yours in quality, price, usefulness, and overall value. You should also request details on various offers and study the sales letters and literature you receive.

Q. *Is a system for getting out of debt a good product to offer by mail?*

A. As long as there are people around, many of them are going to have trouble staying out of debt. According to research figures, more than one million unpaid bills are abandoned every month by people who just move out of town without leaving a forwarding address. Eleven million bad checks also turn up each month. Materials, manuals, and booklets offering a solution to debt are already being sold by mail, but there's plenty of room for new offers. Your own system may be much better than the plans now being sold—your plan may be more helpful, more informative, or more attractive in price.

Q. *With today's increase in violence, would a self-defense product be right for mail order?*

A. Yes. Many self-defense products have been sold by mail for years. Millions of people continue to live in fear, so the market for such items is still large. A recent ad states that a tear gas device called the "paralyzer" can garner sales of $20,000 to $50,000 per year.

Q. *Wouldn't selling full-length books by mail, not short booklets, be a good way to go in mail order?*

A. Actually, more books are reportedly being sold via mail order than in all the nation's bookstores combined (according to *Publishers Weekly*). The big catalog houses that sell to millions of buyer-customers often include at least a few full-length books for sale. Numerous smaller companies offer full-length books on every conceivable subject. This could be a good route for you after you've gained some experience.

Q. *Can a correspondence course be too complicated and expensive to produce and sell by mail?*

A. Yes. I recommend that you wait until you've had some experience in mail order and have had some success with less complicated offers before trying to sell a correspondence course.

SELLING YOUR PRODUCT OR SERVICE

Q. *Can I get started in mail order with one classified ad?*

A. If the ad pulls orders, yes. It's a start, at least. But your profits may be limited.

Q. *If the big money in mail order is in direct mail, why not concentrate on this phase of the business first and skip classified ads completely?*

A. There is money in direct mail all right, but you've got to know what you're doing. The wrong list of names or the wrong sales letter can eat up your money fast. Only a small percentage of those you send sales letters to will send you an order. So it takes bulk mailings to the right lists to get good results. Jumping into direct mail before learning from classified ads is a bit like trying to run before you can walk. It's best to gain experience from classified ads first, and at the same time learn all you can about direct mail.

Q. *When is the best time to send out a direct mailing?*

A. Don't send out any mailing on or near the first of the month. This is when most bills are sent out. Mondays and holidays are also poor days for mail to arrive.

Q. *Does a direct-mail sales letter have to be printed in color?*

A. No. Some of the most effective sales letters are printed in plain black ink on white paper. Color can sometimes pull better for you, but it's usually the content of the sales letter that counts. My first direct-mail sales letter was one page printed in black ink on white paper. And it pulled well for a first letter.

Q. *What is bulk mail?*

A. It's usually thought of to mean high-volume second-, third-, and fourth-class mail and includes packages, magazines, newspapers, catalogs, and circulars. Some mail-order operators also use the term when they send out a lot of first-class letters.

Q. *Where can I get information on bulk mail postage rates and postal regulations that apply to mail order?*

A. The main branch of your local post office can supply you with basic information. One of the quickest ways to get all the postal information you need is to write your congressman or senator and request it.

Q. *In the inquiry and follow-up method of selling, how many extra attempts to land a sale should be made after the prospect fails to send an order from the first attempt?*

A. Veteran mail-order operators say there's no limit. Sales have been made on the fifth, 10th, and 25th try. But this, of course, takes a lot of sales letters. Also, good lists of those who inquire for more details often pull much better than cold lists of names.

Q. *Don't most free offers have a catch?*

A. Yes. If you promote a free offer, be sure that no hidden strings are attached.

Q. *Are a lot of mail-order items returned with a money-back request?*

A. No. Surprisingly, most people do not go to the trouble of returning a product once they've bought and received it. But if an offer turns out to be misleading or false, buyers will return it quickly. The law of fair play seems to rule here. Treat prospects fairly, with genuine and legitimate offers, and you won't have to worry about returns.

Q. *What publications should I read regularly in order to keep up with what's happening in mail order?*

A. You should frequently look over the mail-order sections of *House Beautiful, Selling Direct, Salesman's Opportunity, Popular Science, Popular Mechanics,* the *Wall Street Journal,* and the *New York Times.*

Q. *I'm interested in the entire field of advertising, not just the mail-order branch. Where can I get more information about advertising?*

A. Your best bet is to subscribe to *Advertising Age,* which is the bible of the advertising business. It's published each week. The address is:

> Advertising Age
> 740 North Rush Street
> Chicago, IL 60611

Q. *Can the experience of running a mail-order company lead to a career in some other area of advertising?*

A. Yes. Planning and writing mail-order ads sharpens your copywriting skills. If you like working with copy, you might find a good job as a copywriter with either an advertising agency or an advertiser.

MAIL-ORDER FRAUD

Q. *Are a lot of mail-order offers just dishonest schemes dreamed up by money-hungry individuals?*

A. Yes. But most mail-order operators are honest and offer legitimate items by mail. Every industry has its bad apples, and there are plenty of them in mail order. I was a victim of some of these schemes when I started. I did learn something about dishonest mail offers by being a victim of them, but they also separated me from some of my hard-earned money in the process. There are many honest and valid advertising courses, manuals, and certain books that can help a newcomer to mail order. But be careful. Every year there are more mail-order schemers. If you do order from one of these dishonest companies, you may never receive anything. If you are suspicious of a mail-order company, check with the Better Business Bureau in the area where the company is operating to see if the firm is reputable.

Q. *I've noticed that various pyramid schemes are offered by mail. Are these illegal?*

A. Unfortunately, some unscrupulous mail-order operators continue to offer these schemes. Many schemes are variations on the old chain letter routine. Chain letters are a waste of time and are usually illegal, but some schemers are able to operate on the fringe of the law. Never make any pie-in-the-sky offer that smacks of a pyramid scheme or chain letter. There will always be gullible people who'll try to get something for nothing. But to con them out of their money is the lowest level of ethics and character. Your reputation is one of your most important assets in mail order, so don't drag it in the dirt by using devious advertising. Once a crooked operator is caught using the mail to cheat people, that person may never get the right to sell by mail again. And the laws are getting tougher each year. Selling by mail is a privilege. So run your business on the highest ethical level and treat your customers as you would like to be treated. The Golden Rule has a clear and direct application to the mail-order business. P. T. Barnum, the great promoter of the last century, said it well: "Always try to give people honest value for their money." Following this rule will help to ensure your success in mail order.

SUCCESS STORY: A Kite and Balloons Business Soars to Success

Colin Renwick, a former seaman, has become king of balloons in Britain. His business will do two million pounds this year.

Shipped off to sea as a boy sailor at age 12, Renwick became the boy chief petty officer on the Arethusa, *a steel barque. Colin was lured ashore in the late 1970s to help launch the Kite and Balloon Company, which was then a small shop in South London. Within a few weeks the company was doing 1,000 pounds a week in sales at the store alone. They then expanded into mail order and increased their business even further.*

According to Renwick, there's even more money in staging balloon events and promotions, and in using balloons for decorations at parties of the rich and famous.

5

Choosing Your Product or Service

HOW MAIL ORDER WORKS

Success in mail order often follows a simple pattern. First, a need for a certain product is discovered, and an item is developed and produced to meet that need. Next, the product is tested with a few initial ads offering real value for the buyer's money. The orders received are filled efficiently and promptly. Finally, the business is expanded by increasing the amount of money devoted to advertising. If handled wisely, the increased advertising will bring in a growing number of orders.

The entire idea of a mail-order business might be summed up this way: First, you obtain or create a product or service to sell; second, you find ways to reach prospective customers with information about your product. That's mail order in a nutshell.

WHY PEOPLE BUY BY MAIL

Why do they do it? Why do more and more people send checks and money orders through the mail for all manner of products and services? There are a variety of reasons, and as the operator of your own mail-order business, you should be aware of them. One big reason for buying by mail is convenience. Many stores today seem to care little about a customer's business. In a great many stores today customers are left to wait on themselves. Service is a thing of the past. If you find what you want, that's fine. If you don't, tough luck! That seems to be the attitude of many stores. Times have changed. You might say that the customer is no longer right—at least not in many stores. Shopping by mail eliminates the need to scour a store in search of needed items.

A person who shops by mail often achieves a sense of freedom. No confrontation with a salesperson is necessary. The sales talk is in the ad or in the sales literature received by mail. It can be tossed in the wastebasket or set aside for later consideration. It can also be acted on at once.

The higher-priced products in stores are usually kept under the watchful eye of a salesperson hoping to motivate the customer to take action. Not so with mail order. Buyers are free to decide to buy or not to buy in the comfort and privacy of their own home or apartment. That's freedom—without pressure of any kind.

Another reason for mail-order buying is that buying by mail saves time that would otherwise be spent fighting traffic and coping with parking problems. It's true that many large shopping malls have solved the parking problem to a large extent, but a shopper may want to visit one or more stores not located in a mall. In addition, the malls get crowded on weekends and during holiday periods. Accidents can and do take place, just getting in and out of these huge parking areas.

Retailers have been using the lure of the bargain for years. The chance to save money has pulling power just about everywhere. This lure works wonders in the mail-order business, depending, of course, on what the bargain happens to be. One example is a booklet advertised as "revealing the secrets of a long and healthy life." The asking price was only $1.00. This offer obviously looked like a bargain to many buyers and no doubt did well for the seller.

Another bargain offer advertised recently was the chance to hear again many of the old favorite radio programs and stars of yesteryear. About 1,500 different programs were available on cassettes, tape reels, and cartridges. The price quoted for a catalog listing the programs was $2.00. A strong interest in Depression Era nostalgia items at the time of the offer naturally added to its appeal.

Up to a certain price threshold, impulse buying is an important factor in mail order. The temptation to buy may not be as strong as when a customer is actually in a store and looking at a product, trying it on, admiring it, or whatever. But display ads often show attractive pictures of a product. A well-done display ad can often stimulate a customer's impulse to buy.

Maybe some buyers have just had a bad day, like the sound of the offer, or just want to buy a given item. Let's face it. If people will plunk down cash to buy an impulse item like the book filled with blank pages called *The Nothing Book,* they will buy almost anything. A manual titled *Your Talking Cat* is also selling well. People everywhere often buy a few things just to give themselves a lift. There's no question about it. Impulse buying is here to stay. It goes on in stores every day. And it also brings in orders by mail.

A good example of a special-attraction item is one offered by a company in Tennessee. They are currently advertising and selling wallpaper with over 30 etchings from the boyhood and rise to stardom of Elvis Presley. The wallpaper comes in six colors.

Whether sold in a store, by mail, or both ways, you can clearly see the special attraction of such a product. Product items with a connection to superstars have always sold well and will continue to sell.

Another key reason why so many people buy by mail is that they get a kick out of anticipating the arrival of the item in the mail. It comes addressed to the buyer, so it seems very personal. The buyer can await its arrival with real expectation, a certain amount of excitement, and maybe even a sense of mystery.

It's fun to receive things in the mail. It's also true that many people don't get much mail. The arrival of their order can grow in importance during the time it takes to be shipped and actually received. For many lonely people, the arrival of an anticipated package may be an event that gives them a badly needed lift and feeling of pleasure.

Another reason people buy by mail is the appeal of newness. How does this affect a mail-order business? There are two schools of thought about mail-order products. Some so-called experts recommend that newcomers offer a product that is already being sold successfully by other mail-order operators. Others believe that newcomers might well do better by offering something new.

The number of orders you receive is certainly going to be greatly reduced if dozens of other mail-order operators are offering the same product or item. It used to confuse me when I read in various mail-order instruction materials that the way to proceed was to be a copycat and sell the same items already being offered. The copycat idea is true to a certain degree, but success often depends on what the product actually is and how many others are selling it.

I can tell you for certain, based on my own years of experience in mail order, that some of the items I offered that were also being sold by others proved to be complete duds. I ran good ads for these items in leading mail-order magazines and weekly tabloids, but too many others were selling the same thing or something very similar.

So take the idea of being a copycat with a grain of salt. It might work well for you at times, when not too many others are offering the same thing. But there's no guarantee that you're going to do well, just because others are selling the same item. The competition might very well hurt your own sales. You can, of course, test any doubtful products or items first, to see if the market for them has already been tapped by other mail-order operators.

It's good to remain a little skeptical in your reading about mail order. All kinds of instruction courses and materials concerning mail order are being offered today. Some are good and worth the money; others are not based on real facts. Some of these plans for making money by mail just don't work, as I found out in my early experiences with buying and trying some of them.

On the other hand, there are some sound reasons for offering something new to prospects. New products and offers may be harder to introduce and establish, but many mail-order operators have done well with them over the years. Some of my own products were brand new, and they continue to sell for me.

People like to buy and own something new. It's ingrained in most. It gives them a happy feeling. There's something very basic about the appeal of newness.

OTHER REASONS FOR BUYING BY MAIL

Along with the reasons for buying by mail already given, a few others are worth keeping in mind. An important one is the buyer's belief that the product will be of better quality than is available locally.

Many buyers enjoy owning products that are different in some way. The novelty appeal of a number of mail-order products is very apparent. I well remember sending in cereal box tops, back in the golden days of radio programs, for special products like the Captain Midnight badge and secret decoder. Such highly prized items could be obtained only by mail order. They were unusual and exciting products. The days they arrived in the mail were special ones, especially if you were the first kid on the block to get one.

There's one type of mail-order buyer who has little choice but to do business by mail. These buyers are shut-ins. For many of the elderly, the handicapped, or those homebound for whatever reason, mail order is a real lifesaver. The products and services they need come right to their front doors and mailboxes, saving them considerable hardship.

THE DOMINANT WANTS OF PEOPLE

The reasons why people buy by mail can be traced to one or more of the dominant human wants or desires. Customers will not hesitate to order by mail to fulfill these different wants and desires. A mail-order product that satisfies one or more of these wants will be sought after and bought. The dominant wants of most people are:

- To enjoy oneself
- To be popular
- To be healthy
- To save time
- To escape physical pain
- To be clean
- To attract the opposite sex
- To make money
- To be praised
- To conserve possessions
- To satisfy one's appetite
- To be in style
- To avoid effort
- To save money
- To gratify curiosity
- To avoid trouble
- To be like others
- To avoid criticism
- To protect one's reputation
- To have beautiful possessions
- To be an individual
- To have security
- To be appreciated

- To take advantage of opportunities
- To be secure in buying
- To be important
- To be creative
- To be self-confident
- To be successful
- To have more leisure time
- To have influence over others

A mail-order product that fulfills a combination of these human wants will have a lot going for it. When deciding on a product to sell by mail, refer to this list. A concentrated effort to center your product and selling strategy around several of these mass desires will pay off handsomely. Run down the want list with your product or service. Does it fulfill any of these human desires? If so, how many? Will it sell year-round? For example, a huge industry is built around people's desire to have more romance in their lives. The large profits made year-round in the cosmetics industry is proof that millions of people want to look more attractive.

The Boom in Historical Romances

At this writing, historical romance novels are selling millions of copies. Romance books in general are chalking up new sales records. The reason is quite simple. Millions of people desire romance and will buy books and other products that offer it. Many such books are sold by mail to a seemingly endless market of buyers.

A FABULOUS MAIL-ORDER PRODUCT

Think what a four-star, fabulous mail-order product you would have if it related to all of the dominant wants of most people. Try to offer a product or service that will at least relate to two or three of the key human desires. For example, a product geared to the desire to make money might also include the desire for comfort and security. One Canadian company sells "7 Simple Business Ideas" (documents) for $85.00 per order.

Ask yourself how a product or service you're considering will make a buyer feel happier, more popular, better educated, more stylish, or less tired. Think about human needs and desires. And then try to match them with a product or service you can obtain or produce yourself. It's vital that you keep in mind the way that your chosen product meets these mass desires. When it comes time to plan your product's advertising or sales literature, this information will be very important.

It's the underlying meaning behind a product or service that often makes it irresistible. Take life insurance as an example. Few people want to buy more life insurance on any given day. But the wise person selling life insurance—whether by mail or face-to-face—talks about a secure and satisfying retirement income, a college education for a couple's children, a dream trip to Europe, a second home at the lake, and other tangible desires. These are the things a sound insurance program with a growing cash value over the years can make possible for the buyer. But the words "life insurance" turn many people off. The emphasis should be on the things that life insurance stands for and can make possible.

GET THE TOTAL MARKETING PICTURE

One objective of this book is to help you to see the total marketing picture of the product or service you choose to sell by mail. An understanding of the total marketing picture can considerably increase your chances of success in mail order, even if the product is your very first one.

By the total market picture, I mean packaging, advertising, promotion, merchandising, and selling. You will use advertising and promotion the most in mail order, but some knowledge of the other areas will certainly be of help.

Usually the more you know about your product the more you will sell of it. This is one good reason for originating or producing your mail-order product yourself. By creating it yourself, you will know it better than anyone else. And your special knowledge of it will aid you in advertising and promoting it. According to marketing expert Edwin L. Artzt, "It's very difficult for a competitor to rip off your advertising if your campaign has a real trademark quality to it."

ENTHUSIASM FOR YOUR PRODUCT

One of the first mail-order products that I originated was a book (really a minibook) on how to increase one's creative powers and abilities. I reasoned that this product related to several of the key human desires and could certainly be sold successfully by mail. After I completed the minibook, I discovered that it fulfilled several of the dominant wants:

- the desire to be more creative
- the desire for enjoyment
- the appeal of being an individual (which my product met in several ways)
- the desire to make money (a strong promise of the product)
- the desire to gratify curiosity
- the desire to increase self-confidence (through the act of creating things)
- the desire to express one's personality
- the desire to be an important person

A few of the other key desires were fulfilled indirectly by my product.

I'm happy to report that this minibook is still selling by mail today and has been one of my best products. I use both ads and direct mail to tell prospects about it. Some who have bought the minibook have even taken the time to write to me personally and praise the product. It has, in a number of cases, opened up a whole new way of life for the buyer. It has also added quite a bit to my bank account over the last several years.

I want to emphasize something here—enthusiasm for your product or service. Whatever you offer to buyers by mail, you'll need to be enthusiastic about it. After planning and seeing my original minibook come to life following months of work and development, I found that I was filled with enthusiasm for it. This was a great help in working out the ads, sales letters, and literature for it.

Don't try to offer something by mail that you don't believe in yourself, that you can't see the value of, or that you don't have genuine enthusiasm for. There is real power in enthusiasm. This power can serve as a foundation for your new and growing mail-order business.

START WITH ONE PRODUCT OR SERVICE

I found that one of the most important rules of the mail-order business is that a beginner should start with only one product or service. I can't emphasize this too much. You need to know a lot about the business before trying to sell several products simultaneously.

When you select your first product you want to aim for an item with a hobby or do-it-yourself appeal. Look for something that's different from what's being sold in stores. If you find a product within these guidelines you will be well on your way to a profitable start in mail order. (The appendix at the end of this chapter will give you some ideas for products or services.)

A specialty product is an item that is sold exclusively by the seller. A booklet that you produce, for example, or some other product that you originate and sell yourself would be considered a specialty product.

I did a lot of thinking about what I wanted to sell first. I wanted a simple product that I could have complete control over. I first considered selling a product manufactured by an established company, but I decided that I preferred handling my own item—something I could produce myself.

I studied a number of products that were being sold by mail. I did this by actually answering the ads for a variety of products. When I looked over the sales material and literature on these various offers, I was impressed by the number of informational booklets that were being sold by mail.

INFORMATIONAL BOOKLETS

I did some more checking and discovered that informational booklets of all kinds form one of the main product categories of the mail-order industry. I noticed that ads for these booklets were appearing in most mail-order publications as far back as the 1940s and 1950s. They continued to sell well through the 1980s, with every indication that they'll keep pulling in orders through the rest of the century.

An informational booklet seemed like a good item to start with. I felt certain I could put together one or more that would be helpful to many buyers.

I ordered a number of different booklets by mail, read them carefully, and thought about creating one of my own. In a few weeks, I was busy writing a booklet on the subject of success. I reasoned that a booklet on how to be more successful would appeal to many buyers and sell continually. After about a month's work, I had completed a booklet.

The information field is one of the largest individual phases of mail order. There are definite advantages in beginning with a product of this type. It's easy to get started with and is less of a gamble than most other types of offers. Little money is needed to start, and the chance for a high-profit return is excellent.

A booklet that you create, have printed, and sell by mail does not have to be fancy. The buyer doesn't care what your booklet looks like as long as it's neat and readable. Length is not important either. It's the information in the booklet that counts the most. That is what the buyer wants.

Should you like the idea of producing your own informational booklet as your first product item to sell, it will help you to refer to the following list of book topics that have long proven themselves to be consistent sellers:

1. Self-help
2. Money-making ideas
3. Business opportunities
4. The occult
5. Religion
6. Travel
7. How-to
8. Home businesses
9. Reference

HOW-TO BOOKLETS

Some of the best continuing sellers in the mail-order informational field are how-to booklets. There are bound to be at least a few such subjects that interest you or that you already know something about. With a little time and research, you can easily write up such a booklet. If you don't type, you could farm it out. Word processors with high-quality printers can produce a very professional-looking guide. After the pages have been neatly typed, the next step is to have enough copies of the booklet printed to fill the initial orders you'll receive.

There will always be buyers interested in the do-it-yourself approach. To stimulate your thinking along these lines, some how-to booklets currently being sold by mail include the following titles:

- How to Talk to Your Cat
- How to Stop Smoking

- How to Become a Consultant
- How to Develop Psychic Powers
- How to Become a Coin Dealer
- How to Make Big Money in the Stock Market
- How to Write for Profit
- How to Operate a Charm and Modeling Business
- How to Open Locked Doors Instantly
- How to Raise Rabbits
- How to Lose Weight
- How to Stay Young
- How to Become a Piano Tuner

These are only a few of the hundreds of how-to booklets now being sold. The ads for many of them are continually seen in various mail-order publications, so they must be bringing in orders to the operators. Ads for a given mail-order product don't keep appearing unless they're producing enough orders to realize a good profit.

COPYRIGHT PROTECTION FOR YOUR MATERIAL

If you intend to offer any kind of informational booklet, pamphlet, correspondence course, or similar material by mail order, some general understanding of copyright law is necessary.

When you create certain materials, you automatically acquire certain rights. The best way to understand a copyright is to think of it as a form of protection provided through the law of a country to authors of literary, artistic, musical, dramatic, or other intellectual works.

A separate or individual copyright must be obtained for each work, in order to have full protection.

Exclusive Rights

The owner of the copyright has the exclusive rights:

1. to reproduce the copyrighted work in copies or phonorecords
2. to prepare derivative works based on the copyrighted work
3. to distribute copies or phonorecords of the copyrighted work to

the public by sale or other transfer of ownership, or by rental, lease, or lending

4. in the case of literary, musical, dramatic, and choreographic works, pantomimes, and motion pictures and other audiovisual works, to perform the copyrighted work publicly

5. in the case of literary, musical, dramatic, and choreographic works, pantomimes, and pictorial, graphic, or sculptural works, including the individual images of a motion picture or other audiovisual work, to display the copyrighted work publicly

Subject Matter of Copyright

The following types of material can be copyrighted. This is not a complete list, but it will give you a good idea of the range.

Copyright protection subsists, in accordance with this title, in original works of authorship fixed in any tangible medium of expression, now known or later developed, from which they can be perceived, reproduced, or otherwise communicated, either directly or with the aid of a machine or device. Works of authorship include the following categories:

1. literary works (see attached definition)
2. musical works, including any accompanying words
3. dramatic works, including any accompanying music
4. pantomimes and choreographic works
5. pictorial, graphic, and sculptural works
6. motion pictures and other audiovisual works
7. sound recordings

In no case does copyright protection for an original work of authorship extend to any idea, procedure, process system, method of operation, concept, principle, or discovery, regardless of the form in which it is described, explained, illustrated, or embodied in such work.

The following cannot be copyrighted:

1. Titles
2. Short phrases, names, slogans, and familiar symbols or designs
3. Plans, ideas, methods, devices, or systems
4. Blank forms used as time cards, diaries, bank checks, address books, report forms, and account books

5. Information that is not of original authorship—common knowledge—such as sports event schedules, height-weight charts, and tape measures

The Copyright Notice

Once copies have been produced and a work has been published, a copyright notice must appear on each copy. The notice consists of three required elements:

1. The name of the copyright owner or owners
2. The year the work was published
3. The word "Copyright," its abbreviation "Copr.," or the symbol ©

Here is an example of the correct use of this required notice:

© Bill Brown

For a book or material published in book form, the notice should go on the title page or on the page following it (the reverse side of the title page).

Unpublished works do not have to include the notice, according to law. But it would be wise to have it on any copies, so the work can't be mistakenly published without notice.

Changes in the Copyright Law

In January 1978, a Copyright Revision Bill replaced the old law. Here are some of the law's changes:

1. Copyright protection of a work lasts for the author's lifetime plus 50 years. This applies to any work created after January 1, 1978. Works already copyrighted before 1978 can now be renewed for an additional 47 years, rather than the period of 28 years specified in the old law.
2. The new law has raised the royalty on music recordings from 2¢ to 2¾¢ or ½¢ per minute of playing time, whichever amount is larger.
3. The operators of jukeboxes must now pay royalties for music used.

4.   Published or unpublished works are now covered by the U.S. copyright law.

A full copy of the copyright law may be obtained from the Copyright Office in Washington, D.C. Highlights and summary information on various aspects of the new changes are also available in circulars R99 and R15a from the same office.

Steps in Securing a Copyright

1.   Write the Register of Copyrights at the following address:

Register of Copyrights
Library of Congress
Washington, D.C. 20559

2.   Request the application form for the type of work you wish to copyright.

3.   Complete the application form for whatever you wish to register and return with the requested fee and copies of the work.

4.   Your certificate of copyright will be mailed to you in several weeks. Keep it in a safe place.

MANY BIG SELLERS ARE STILL SIMPLE ITEMS

One clear fact you need to stay aware of when thinking about mail-order products is that many big sellers in the business are still basically simple items.

In the toy area, for example, the market is currently glutted with toys that are too smart. In truth, a great many families and prospective toy buyers want simple, creative toys without a set function. If toys do everything for children, their creativity and imagination are never stimulated.

There's no question that the big sellers of the toy world are still simple ones. According to a representative of the Toy Manufacturers of America, the more popular toys are Hot Wheels cars, the classic Barbie doll, play kitchens, and Teenage Mutant Ninja Turtle action figures. A great learning toy is the Solar Wooden Model Kit. Children eight and older can make an easy-to-put-together solar-powered airplane, helicopter, or windmill. The price is $18 from Real Goods of Uklah, California.

Quality Algarve bedspreads are still selling well by mail. So are T-shirts, pipes, mailbox covers, manuals on raising business capital, teddy bears, mailing lists, and a host of other products and services.

The point to remember is that simple items can keep selling for years. A product or service need not be a technical, complicated item to do well on the market.

Books continue to sell very well via mail order. You can get the names of book companies wanting dealers in mail-order magazines like *Selling Direct* and *Salesman's Opportunity*. Ads for book dealers appear regularly in most issues. You can write to the companies for the details of their dealership arrangements and compare your potential profits. Reading some of the mail-order publications regularly will supply you with the names of many book companies that would be glad to have you as a dealer. A special advantage of selling books is that they appeal to all ages. The potential market is enormous.

SELLING A SERVICE

If you prefer to sell a service, do some thinking about how you might help people in some way. Perhaps you have some special type of knowledge that you could use in a mail-order service. Consider your background. Almost every person is good at something or has special knowledge about one subject or another. Think about your hobbies, interests, and talents. You might find several possibilities for services you could offer by mail. This might be the best approach for you in mail order. For example, people who are experienced in advertising have used their ability to start an advertising service. I've done this myself and now serve a number of national clients as an advertising consultant. This is in addition to the products I sell by mail order.

A WARNING ABOUT OVERSTOCKING

Whatever product you come up with, don't overstock the item at first. Wait until you've had a chance to test your product out with ads in key mail-order publications. Once you have an item that is pulling in orders consistently and allows you a healthy profit after your expense in producing, stocking, and shipping it to buyers, you can then stock all you need to fill incoming orders. Many newcomers to mail order have fallen into the trap of overstocking their product only to find out later that not enough orders come in to deplete the stock on hand. Test first for an initial response to your ad, and when your product looks like a winner, you can then increase your stock accordingly.

YOU CAN SELL SOMEONE ELSE'S PRODUCT

If you prefer not to originate a product yourself, you can still get into mail order by selling an existing product. There are numerous product suppliers that will drop-ship their items to your mail-order customers. In order to use this method, you must send your customer's order (with the name and address of the buyer typed on a label that has your company name on it) to the supplier. You get orders by running your own ads or sales letters.

The names and addresses of various product suppliers can be found in mail-order magazines, classified telephone directories, statewide industrial directories, and other special directories found in most public libraries.

KNOW THE MARKET FOR YOUR PRODUCT

Whatever the product, service, or offer you start off with, do some careful thinking about the market for it. Try to determine who your prospects are and their approximate age. If you're trying to reach teenagers and young people, for example, certain publications would be better than others. If senior citizens are your main target, special publications for older people would be best suited for your ads.

Take plenty of time deciding what your first product or offer will be. It's a vital decision. Choosing the right product to sell is considered the most important requirement for success in mail order.

Soon after World War II, one man hit upon the idea of selling cuckoo clocks. He imported them from a manufacturer he met while serving in the army in Germany. These cuckoo clocks were the first product choice of Brainerd Mellinger. The clocks sold well by mail. Today Mellinger is an internationally known trader and businessman. He says that he owes every penny of his fortune to mail order.

THINKING AHEAD

Thinking ahead can make a big difference in your business. After you choose your first product, you will need to line up a reliable supplier— unless you plan to produce it yourself. Then you must create your ads and determine the best times to run them. Much advance thinking and planning are called for in mail order. Thinking ahead is really a small price to pay for substantial and lasting success.

DROP-SHIP ARRANGEMENTS

If you prefer to sell an existing product rather than produce your own, then the key word to keep in mind is "drop-ship." A drop-ship is an arrangement in which manufacturers offer their products to you at a special discount price and ship the items directly to your customers. All that you're usually required to supply are the payment for the order and a completed shipping label. A company that agrees to work with you will explain any other necessary requirements.

It is important to communicate with any manufacturer you contact in a professional way. If you write to leading manufacturers in longhand and without using a letterhead, they probably won't reply. They want to deal only with serious-minded individuals who conduct their business in a professional manner. So be sure to type all letters to manufacturers on your letterhead.

The profit potential of a drop-ship arrangement is good. If you can buy an item from a manufacturer for $3.00 or $4.00 and then sell it to your customers for $8.00 or $9.00, your profits will add up. In most cases, the profit margin is very high. Many manufacturers will offer a larger discount than you'd usually receive from a wholesaler, allowing you a higher profit margin.

Setting Up a Drop-Ship Agreement

There are many manufacturers of a variety of products that are willing to drop-ship for mail-order companies. Here are some proven tips to help you set up a drop-ship agreement with a manufacturer.

1. Look through trade journals and directories for the names of leading manufacturers. The Yellow Pages also list many manufacturers.

2. Write to manufacturers on your business letterhead. Type all of your letters and keep copies.

3. State your willingness to pay for your first product purchases in advance. Perhaps you can establish credit later, after you've placed several orders.

4. Try to be as businesslike as possible. If you're writing to request details about a particular product, enclose a self-addressed, stamped envelope (one of your business envelopes).

5. Explain in your letter that you wish to offer your mail-order customers new products of value, and that you believe that their company has such a product. Ask for descriptive material on the products you like and what the discount price will be to you as a mail-order dealer. Close your letter with a request for a quick reply.

Special Sources for Drop-Ship Selling

By using some special sources found in most large libraries, you can find a number of good drop-ship manufacturers to contact. Two of the best sources for manufacturers are *McCrae's Blue Book* and *Thomas's Register of American Manufacturers*. Both are large and accurate directories listing the name, address, and specific products of all leading U.S. manufacturers. Other countries have similar directories or trade journals in which key manufacturers are listed.

A STRONG REASON TO BE ENTHUSED ABOUT MAIL ORDER

According to the Census Bureau there will be a whopping 300 million people in the United States alone by the year 2000. The population in most other countries is also growing. This means a huge and ever-growing number of customers to buy your mail-order products and services. I've done well, myself, with self-improvement products. So keep the golden potential of self-help books, products, and services in mind. Find or develop a product or service you can start with. Begin planning now to get your slice of this billion dollar mail-order pie.

Appendix to Chapter 5

Product Ideas and Advice to Get You Started

MAIL-ORDER PRODUCT IDEAS

A study of the mail-order industry shows that many people enter the business with either a booklet or a specialty or novelty item. Quite a few of these mail-order operations are doing a healthy business today selling the same basic product that they started with. Some of the following items are now being offered; others are new ideas that might work well for you. Some are more suitable for mail order than others. All of them will stimulate your thinking about products.

Old Records.   Buy old LP (long-playing) records and sell them to music lovers for a profit. Many record buyers don't wish to pay the high prices of today's compact discs.

Elvis Presley Materials.   These could include written tributes to the late singer, a short booklet of poems about Elvis, facts about his life collected and printed in a special momento-style form, or even a recorded tape message about Elvis. Even Elvis toothbrushes are sold. In some cases, however, special permission might have to be obtained to sell Elvis-related items.

Another idea for an Elvis-related offer is a correspondence course about the great entertainer. It would take some time to develop, but it might be tremendously profitable. You would have to decide how many parts to include in your course and the length of each. Millions of Elvis fans all over the world might respond warmly to a well-done course about the life of the king of rock and roll. There was an actual course on Elvis offered at the University of Tennessee at Knoxville. It has since evolved into a course on the history of rock and roll, but it shows that the interest is there.

Conservation Kits. These could include a checklist or pamphlet of 50 or more ways to save energy and conserve on cooling, heating, and refrigeration. Millions are very interested in such information, so your sales could be very good.

Do-It-Yourself Divorce Kits. This item has been sold successfully in some states. With the skyrocketing divorce rate, there's no doubt that a huge market is still out there for such an item. You could tailor your divorce kit to the divorce laws of your country or home state.

A former barber in Rochester, New York, hit on a clever new way to make money. Not long ago, he was selling do-it-yourself divorce kits for $75.00 each and "separation" kits for $25.00. The kits included all the required forms and information on the procedures necessary to obtain a divorce or separation in the state of New York.

If sold in other states, each kit would, of course, have to provide the correct forms for that particular location. By meeting the requirements of each state, the kits could probably be sold everywhere.

Over a million divorces are obtained each year in the United States alone, so demand for the kits should be quite strong. The fact that many lawyers charge $700 or more for a divorce strengthens the demand even more. Certain age groups seem to have a higher divorce rate than others. For the group under 34, the divorce rate is presently double what it was only 10 years ago. This group might be a good target for your ads.

Guidance Services for Retired People. Millions of retired people have little or no idea of where to retire. You could do some research on a list of communities or retirement villages in your area, rating them on the basis of such factors as quality and relative cost.

There are other ways to help retired people. Vacation guides, health protection tips, and information on Social Security benefits are a few items of interest to the retirement set. Material on interesting things for retired people to do could also be produced and offered. A lot of retired people don't know what to do with all their time.

Special Information Booklets for Teenagers. A strong possible title might be "What Every Teenager Should Know." The information could cover all kinds of useful facts that would be helpful to teens. Mailing-list brokers can provide you with a huge number of teenage prospects (see Chapter 9). Estimates indicate that teenagers spent $30 billion in 1982 on all types of products.

Guides to the National Parks.   Camping is big business. Millions everywhere hit the trail for the great outdoors every season. Why not offer them a special guide to the national parks and key camping areas of your country? This product could be a year-round mail-order seller because families and camping enthusiasts are always thinking about their next trip.

Special Newsletters for Selected Markets.   These might vary in length from just two pages to 10 or more. The idea is to decide on the market that you want to reach in advance. Who would be the best or most likely prospects for a newsletter? Families might buy a newsletter if the material in it helped or informed them. Child guidance tips might sell and be very welcome. One possibility might be to tell families how they can keep from worrying about their children.

Fortunes have been made from popular newsletters. Years ago, one enterprising man launched a 14-page weekly newsletter. He promoted it and watched it grow to more than 8,000 copies a week. Today, this former newsletter has become a newspaper and is the largest conservative organ in the United States. The publication, known as *Human Events,* has a current weekly circulation over 80,000.

Special Lists.   One of the top best-selling books of recent years was *The Book of Lists.* Directories have sold well for many years. Why not think about compiling lists of prospects, unusual companies, or anything else that others might find useful? Then offer the lists by mail for a fair price.

Booklets on Reincarnation, Astrology, or Some Aspect of the Occult.   People never seem to tire of reading and speculating about the world of the occult. Raymond Moody's book on immortality, *Life After Life,* has sold millions of copies. The occult offers all kinds of product and service possibilities. Even mediums are selling their own books and materials by mail.

Sports Equipment Items.   You might be able to come up with some accessories connected with this product area. Consider this idea carefully. Ask yourself what could help tennis players, boat owners, or joggers.

Tests.   People everywhere are curious by nature. All kinds of tests (forms to be filled in or questions to be answered) are therefore worth considering. People enjoy answering test questions and adding up their scores. You could easily come up with a winner here. A number of tests are now being sold, but there's certainly room for more. The cost of having test forms printed is low, so the profit margin is good.

Clothes Accessories. A study done by the research department of *Seventeen* magazine, on apparel spending by teenage American girls, revealed that the total estimated annual amount spent on *all* apparel is $18 billion.

Recorded Sounds. Amazing as it may seem, there are now records of whale and bird sounds. And they sell.

Tape Cassette Messages. Perhaps you can tell others how to do something. If so, you might sell tape-recorded messages. Plan for about 120 spoken words a minute when recording.

Speed Reading and Self-Improvement Courses. These could be done in the form of a booklet, record, or tape. People everywhere are reading more than ever. A great many readers would like to be able to read much faster while maintaining good comprehension.

Many people are very responsive to self-improvement courses. Show them how your course can help them, and you're going to make a lot of sales. Many individuals dislike the work they do for a living. Millions of workers around the globe are looking for a better and more profitable future. Convince them that your product or service can help them to get ahead, and you'll make money.

Loneliness Market Items. This market alone could make you rich. Loneliness is destroying a lot of people these days.

Anyone can feel lonely. Could you offer a product or service that would help lonely people? Maybe you could come up with something to prevent loneliness or help people to cope with it. You might do the world a great service and get rich besides.

Money Savers. Prospects will pay well for items that show them how to get more for their money.

One man in California actually figured out a way to live fairly well on as little as $4,000 a year. He buys everything at bargain prices and doesn't drive a car at all, but he claims his system works. He said that he has never been happier: "I've left the rat race for good."

Do-It-Yourself Auto Repair Guides. Your offer could range from a handy guidesheet to a full-length manual. This is a recession-proof item that could sell for you all year long.

Things to Sell at Flea Markets. Why not compile a list of popular flea markets and items that could be sold at them? There should be a market for such a source list, and it wouldn't take you long to start selling it.

Handwriting Analysis Services. There are reports of people earning handsome profits from this type of service. Customers mail you a sample of their writing for analysis.

Mind Control Products and Systems. This idea covers manuals, guidesheets, records, tapes, booklets, test forms, and complete correspondence courses.

Menu Services. Plan menus for six months or a year and sell them by mail. One woman is reported to be earning over $75,000 a year making menus.

Guides on How to Winterize Pets. Dogs, cats, and other pets feel the bitter cold of winter too. You might consider producing a manual or simple pamphlet telling pet owners how to keep their dogs and cats warm until another spring rolls around.

Literary Agencies. Sell the articles, stories, newspaper features, and books of aspiring writers to international magazines, newspapers, syndicates, and book publishers. A 10 percent commission rate is standard, but some agents also charge a reading fee for their service.

Movie Posters and Pictures. Some mail-order companies have done well offering these items. You can offer such a variety that your first buyers are very likely to be repeat customers.

Flags. This item calls for special mention. Sales of American flags skyrocketed after the last flag burning received national media coverage. The Desert Storm war also brought sales up considerably. This product should continue to sell well for some time to come.

Herbs and Spices.

Cookbooks. While buyers of these books have become more selective, sales have remained strong. It helps if some unique angle can be used to make the book stand out.

Wigs.

Belts and Unusual Buckles.

Music Boxes.

Car Theft Alarms.

Garden Seeds and Plants.

Audio Tapes for Home and Car. An increasing number of audio tape buyers enjoy listening to a variety of recordings while driving to work or on weekend travels.

Portable Clothes Lines. The sales features are convenience and adaptability.

Hair Grooming Aids.

Gloves of All Types.

Cleaning Services of All Kinds.

Reports That Help People in Some Way. A Kansas company, for example, offers a report on "How to Borrow Money from a Bank." A former banker wrote this report, but it would be a simple matter for you to talk to officials in several banks about the various methods of borrowing. You could also get more information from the Government Printing Office in Washington, D.C. Then take the material and do your own version on borrowing from banks. You might make a small (or large) fortune selling such a report by mail. Whenever the economy takes a plunge, you should easily double or triple your sales.

Writing Improvement Items. Books filled with hundreds of model letters are being sold by mail. Other books and printed material on mistakes in English, and how to correct them, are also currently on the market.

Loan Sources.

Computer Portrait Business. Some companies offering this item are reportedly doing well.

Cable TV Converters. The cable television industry has spawned a variety of products and services now being offered by mail order.

"Tax Secrets" Book.

Solar Radio.

Coonskin Hats. This product seems to be making a comeback (at least via mail order).

Family Wild Game Recipes.

Grocery Coupon Program.

Real Estate Appraiser Course.

T-Shirt Printing Machines.

Hi-Tech Boomerangs.

Portable Sawmill.

Adult Airguns.

Laser-Related Products.

Door Chain Alarms.

"Cold Room" Remedy—Airflow Booster.

Patent/Trademark Information (for inventors).

Auto-Announcer (for detecting visitors).

Loan Broker Information. This item has been selling via mail order for years. The companies continue to run their ads so they must be receiving orders.

Dome Home and Cabin Plans.

Water-Powered Watch.

Metal Recycling.

Folding Chair Plans.

Bumpersticker Printer.

Booklets on How to Clean or Repair Fax Machines.

Loan Sources.

Assembling Sports Equipment at Home.

How to Become a Private Investigator.

Quick-Shine Shoe Sponge.

Piano-Tuning Course.

How to Get Paid for Reading Books.

Home Study Courses on Writing Short Paragraphs for Money. This product has been selling well for many years. Orders are obtained mostly through classified ads. Those who see the ads write in for free details on the course. Follow-up sales literature is then sent.

Records That Teach Self-Hypnosis. Here is another good seller by mail. When the owner of this product first advertised, he was flooded with orders and made a large profit. This record is still selling, evidently, because the ad is continually seen in many leading mail-order publications.

Gadgets and Instructional Materials for Learning the Guitar. These products range from simple instructional booklets to full-length courses and devices, all of which can help one learn the basic chords on the guitar. There are products and booklets for both beginners and experienced guitarists.

Products for Pets. Don't forget that many pets are treated better than human beings. Pet-oriented products are here to stay, since millions of people will probably always have pets and buy all kinds of things for them. Just a few of these pet items include doghouses, dog collars, dog and cat play-toys, pet certificates, and pet clothing items.

Magnifying Eyeglasses. This simple product has been a good seller for years. Many people today are living longer and there's a steady ever-growing market for this kind of item. Magnifying eyeglasses are sold year-round for personal use or as a gift item. Products that only sell well at certain times—such as at Christmas—are naturally limited. Try to pick a product that will sell at any time of year.

Mailbox Covers. This item has been consistently advertised in the mail-order shopping pages of *House Beautiful* magazine for many years. The major appeal of mailbox covers is their immediate usefulness to the buyer.

Hobbies. Many profitable mail-order companies have been built around hobbies. Coin and stamp collecting are two good examples. One mail-order businessman does well by offering a stamp investment counseling service. Stamps and coins have been offered through mail order for decades. Mail-order companies also sell autographs and letters of famous people, matchbooks, postcards, war souvenirs, and other collectibles. So give some thought to possible product-hobby tie-ins.

Bar Lamps and Accessories. Some mail-order firms specialize in this type of merchandise. Bar accessories are usually sold by direct mail, but bar lamps are sometimes sold by display ads. Some companies have sold hundreds of thousands of dollars worth of these bar items.

Boots for Outdoorsmen. The L. L. Bean Company, the largest mail-order firm in New England, began its business in 1912 with this product. The L. L. Bean Company catalog also offers colonial furniture, general store products, and equipment for skiing. A catalog is a worthy goal to strive for, but it takes time, experience, and a growing line of proven sellers to develop a good catalog. A catalog that will consistently produce orders can be a virtual goldmine.

Colonial-Style Bookracks and Pipe Stands. These products are sold successfully by a well-known mail-order company called Yield House. An interesting point to remember is that many mail-order firms in New England began their businesses with products that had a definite tie-in with that section of the country. Maybe you can think of a product or service that would have special appeal to potential customers in the area where you live. Keep it in mind. It could result in a new and profitable product for you.

Novelty Items. Products in this category are different from what can be found in stores today. Jokes, magic tricks, and handmade and imported products are good examples. Remember the hula hoop? When it hit the market its novelty appeal was enormous. There was nothing else like it and sales were in the millions. One of the best bits of advice to guide you in your mail-order business is this: Try to develop a product that will have mass appeal. Any item that satisfies the ambitions, basic desires, and needs of many people is a good choice for your first mail-order product.

Boutique Items. By inscribing words, names, phrases, figures, and cartoon characters on napkins, handkerchiefs, savings banks, wallets, gloves, shirts, jackets, towels, and similar items, they can be turned into something special and unusual. Ask yourself what might be added to an existing product to give it a new effect and appeal. With a little imagination, even an ordinary item like a napkin can be turned into a fine product. This adding-something-new-to-make-it-more-unusual idea can open up many new product possibilities for you.

Art Supplies. As long as there are people interested in sketching, drawing, and painting, art supplies will continue to sell. Buying by mail is easy and inexpensive.

Toys and Games. These have sold steadily since the early days of mail order. Toys and games sell best during the Christmas season; but with effective ads and sales literature, they can be sold throughout the year. Maybe you could dream up a new game. Until you've gained more experience in mail order, though, it is usually safer to offer a tried and tested one.

Religious Items. These include candles, cards, Bibles, bookmarks, framed prayers and religious sayings, and pictures of biblical figures. To get an idea of what is available, visit Christian bookstores, which usually sell a variety of religious items. Also, look over the ads offering religious items in mail-order publications.

Gifts. These continue to be consistent sellers in mail order. There are mail-order companies that have developed complete catalogs of gift items. These catalogs are advertised by direct mail and sometimes by classified and display ads. The increasing number of gift stores is one clear sign of the profitability of mail-order gift items. Many gift stores— which acquire stock through mail order—also sell by it. Many gift manufacturers will drop-ship orders to your customers. Some people have become millionaires and many others have increased their income by selling mail-order gifts.

Baby and Bridal Items. Consider the millions of families with babies, and you will see the excellent profit potential for these products. Bridal items—which include gifts for weddings, engagements, and showers—also represent a possibility for mail-order sales.

Do-It-Yourself Kits. These products enable people to redecorate, clean, install, repair, or do some other activity on their own. Look over some mail-order ads to see what types are currently being offered. Do-it-yourself kits will always have appeal. Many people will continue to want to fix, construct, sharpen, mold—or whatever—themselves.

Camping, Sports, and Recreation Items. Millions of people everywhere dream about their next camping trip. Camping equipment ranges from basic gear to expensive items. Sleeping bags, backpacks, cooking gear, and special clothing are just a few possibilities you might keep in mind. Camping is the most popular type of vacation, and you might just be able to cash in on this interest via mail order.

Toy Balloons. His first display ad for toy balloons brought mail-order millionaire E. Joseph Cossman thousands of dollars. Greatly encouraged, he invested more money in advertising and sold close to $500,000 worth of the balloons in one year alone.

Dolls.   Some mail-order firms have done amazingly well selling inexpensive and unique dolls at bargain prices. Doll tie-ins with films are popular and sell well.

There you have them. These types of product items have done well for their owners, and many of them are still being sold successfully. Perhaps one of these categories will be the key to your own first product selection and a successful start in mail order. Refer to this list often for product ideas. Ask yourself what each category suggests in the way of a product or service. Focus on those product categories that interest and excite you the most.

ADVICE AS YOU BEGIN

Plan for Tomorrow's Prosperity

Over half the members of the Academy of Women Achievers of the New York City YWCA (among them the presidents and vice presidents of various companies) earn over $50,000 a year. Their advice for success is as follows: "Set your goals high and keep climbing." Their specific tips include:

- Get as much education as possible.
- Plan and reevaluate your next goals.
- Work hard.
- Live a balanced life as much as possible.
- Take risks in your business.
- Don't fear responsibility.
- Be assertive, not aggressive.
- Keep your emotions off the job.

In order to achieve the level of success these women represent, it's important to know what you're going to do during troubled economic times. Recessions drain a lot of your energy and can lead to increasing worry unless you have a plan. Many veteran mail-order companies prepare for the return of prosperous times by making consistent plans for it.

Keep this in mind as you decide what products and services to sell by mail.

Think about New Products and Businesses

What new businesses will exist at the turn of the century? What new mail-order products, services, and novelty items will catch the consumer's fancy, meet a new need (or an old one in a better way), and spin off a variety of new businesses? Staying open to new possibilities only makes good sense.

One key to prosperity is to recognize changes and trends. An example is the changing work force. More and more people are working at home these days, including lawyers, clerical personnel, engineers, consultants, editors, writers, architects, and others. In many cases, these people are running their own businesses, or remaining linked to their employers via computers.

So what is the significance of an increase in the work-at-home segment? One certainty is that these people will need office equipment for their homes. Laser printers, computers, fax machines, word processors, electronic typewriters, and related equipment will have a new market. New ideas for selling to this group by mail, or otherwise, will be on target.

Sources of New Business Ideas

Keep the following common sources of new businesses in mind:

- Natural spin-offs from already existing businesses
- Ideas from research and development departments
- Suggestions from associates and business leaders
- Accident

Don't minimize or ignore the role of accident in the development of new product or business ideas. Entrepreneurs occasionally stumble upon very good new business ideas. They may be in the process of looking for other information, or working on something quite different, when—Presto!—a fresh, bright, and potentially terrific idea presents itself.

Stay Incurably Curious

Curious digging can benefit you in your work. The more you can learn about mail order, the better your chance to advance. By just learning a single useful mail-order fact each day, for 365 days, you'll acquire an amazing amount of information that can be consistently helpful to you.

Communications researcher Robert T. Oliver says that today "there is more than a hundred times as much to learn as fifty years ago." To keep up with fast-changing developments and new concepts, one is forced to be more curious—or risk falling behind.

The legendary Henry Ford, in his young working years at an auto factory, became curious about the idea of building a cheaper car that would still offer dependable transportation for the mass public. After working all day in the factory, Ford stayed up late into the night developing his early Ford models. His curiosity paid off big. Of course, he had to follow through with years of work; but it all began because he was curious.

Another modern example of curiosity in action is Richard Marcus, a pianist and former musical director of the Royal Winnipeg Ballet. When Marcus traveled, he watched closely for peanut butter "the way it used to be." He rarely found any he liked.

So what did Marcus do? He started making his own peanut butter at home and gave occasional jars of it to friends, his piano students, and his dentist. In the early 1970s he began selling it from the back of his car. Today, Marcus and his six-member production staff distribute his peanut butter to major supermarkets. "Ten percent of the sales come from mail order," he says, and this part of the business is growing. His customers suggested that he sell his peanut butter by mail when they couldn't find the product in local stores. Marcus calls his product "Crazy Richard's Peanut Butter."

The years pass too swiftly to ignore the need to plan ahead. The growth of your mail-order company, and its prosperity in the early years of the twenty-first century, depend upon how well you do your planning today.

You may not have time for planning every day; but try not to let a single week pass without a scheduled period for planning. Watch for new trends; keep up with what other companies are successfully offering by mail; and always stay alert for new product-service ideas and improvements.

Also: Regularly consider the suggestions from your customers. Remember that one big idea, the right idea for you and your mail-order business, can bring you growth and success beyond your dreams. It can happen to you.

Part II

ADVERTISING

SUCCESS STORY: Direct Mail Financial Advisory Service

Gypsy Kemp runs a direct-mail financial advisory service from her ranch in New Mexico. She got started, back in 1975, by running a classified ad just to see what the results might be. Her first ad cost her $184.00 and it pulled such a large response that she continued to advertise her service. Her business now grosses more than a quarter of a million dollars each year. Gypsy spends only four hours a day operating her business. The rest of the time she relaxes with her family or friends or goes skiing.

6

Advertising Your Product

Before we take a specific look at mail-order advertising, it will help to understand some key points about advertising in general. Advertising is big business, and it is growing by leaps and bounds.

Rosser Reeves, in *Reality in Advertising*, states that advertising "is merely a substitute for a personal sales force." Advertising is a huge industry, employing copywriters, artists, media people, account executives (glorified sales staff), research personnel, and general office workers. Advertising has been flourishing and expanding for over 100 years. For at least the rest of the twentieth century, further boom is predicted for the industry.

The lights burn late on Madison Avenue and also in thousands of other offices around the world. Someone must work late to get a new ad finished, rewrite a radio or television commercial, or dream up a new campaign theme that will increase sales for any one of thousands of products or services.

Many of the hardest working people in advertising are copywriters. They write the copy for print ads, radio and television commercials, and billboards. They often originate the campaign ideas or themes that help put a product in the mind of the consumer. Copy is king in advertising and remains the vital link in moving the goods and services of a nation.

THE HERITAGE OF ADVERTISING

The American College Dictionary defines advertising as "the act or practice of bringing anything, as one's wants or one's business, into public notice, especially by paid announcements in periodicals, on billboards, etc., or on the radio."

Advertising dates back to primitive culture. The precise time when the printed word began to be used in advertising is unknown. But we do know—from evidence in the British Museum—that an Egyptian once advertised for the return of a runaway slave. Various contests, events, and gladiatorial games were advertised in ancient Rome.

Much of the early advertising got out of hand. There was a lack of ethics. Many false claims appeared. Through the centuries, though, advertising has matured and become what is now one of the solid pillars of free enterprise.

THE LEGENDARY CLAUDE HOPKINS

Anyone worth their salt in advertising knows about the remarkable Claude Hopkins. He was one of the greatest and most successful advertising men of this century. Hopkins was motivated by one dominant drive in all the advertising he created: to sell; to move the product. His book, *Scientific Advertising* (Crown, 1966), written in 1923, became the copywriting bible of the advertising business.

The accomplishments of Hopkins are legendary. By far the most effective copywriter of his time, he made a fortune. He skyrocketed Schlitz beer to the top of the American market in a way that showed cleverness and an understanding of psychology. His advertising focused on the fact that the Schlitz bottles were "cleaned with live steam."

Today, many years after the appearance of Hopkins and his book, the great majority of people in advertising still agree with his basic conclusions. Hopkins believed that a test campaign can answer almost any question quickly and cheaply; that the only purpose of advertising is to make sales; that ad writers shouldn't try to be amusing; and that introducing a personality into an ad can make a product famous.

Hopkins felt that advertising is much like the game of chess. He was convinced that a smart copywriter does not attack a rival, but shows the bright side of his product. He tells people what to do, not what to avoid.

He warned of a trap that some copywriters fall into at one time or

Somewhere West of Laramie

SOMEWHERE west of Laramie there's a broncho-busting, steer-roping girl who knows what I'm talking about. She can tell what a sassy pony, that's a cross between greased lightning and the place where it hits, can do with eleven hundred pounds of steel and action when he's going high, wide and handsome.

The truth is—the Playboy was built for her.

Built for the lass whose face is brown with the sun when the day is done of revel and romp and race.

She loves the cross of the wild and the tame.

There's a savor of links about that car—of laughter and lilt and light—a hint of old loves—and saddle and quirt. It's a brawny thing—yet a graceful thing for the sweep o' the Avenue.

Step into the Playboy when the hour grows dull with things gone dead and stale.

Then start for the land of real living with the spirit of the lass who rides, lean and rangy, into the red horizon of a Wyoming twilight.

JORDAN MOTOR CAR COMPANY, Inc., Cleveland, Ohio

This is one of the great ads of all time. It was a completely new approach to selling cars.

another: "The only purpose of advertising is to make sales. Ad writers forget they are salesmen and try to be performers. Instead of sales, they seek applause. Don't try to be amusing. Money spending is a serious matter. The more you tell the more you sell."

THE COPYWRITER OF TODAY

To a large extent, today's advertising is psychology in action. Back in the late 1960s, entertainer and advertising genius Stan Freberg shook up the airline industry with his unheard of concept of admitting in ads that many people feel nervous when flying. One of his print ads, for example, showed a nervous executive on a plane about to be airborne. The headline read, "Hey there, you with the sweaty palms." Freberg could have used the same old tired approach. Instead, he brought new honesty into airline advertising by saying that some people don't enjoy flying and get nervous.

Today's modern copywriter must keep in mind that there is a real connection between advertising and psychology. A good knowledge of human nature can be very helpful in motivating people to buy various products. Curiosity, for example, is an important tool for a copywriter. Puffed Wheat and Puffed Rice cereals attained success largely through their appeal to the curious. The ad slogan "Foods shot from guns" led both cereals to enjoy substantial sales.

There is a great deal of respect today for the intelligent use of psychology in advertising. In general, motivational research is simply the systematic study of why consumers do what they do—why they buy certain products and shun others. Such studies attempt to correlate the buyer's needs, desires, emotions, and actions. The reasons why consumers buy given products, patronize certain businesses, support specific candidates, and choose the goods and services they do stem from human nature itself. By compiling data on what appeals to consumers, motivational research helps the salesperson find the most effective way to approach the consumer. The following references may give you new ideas for products and advertising appeals as well as some valuable insights into consumer motivation:

- Boyd, Harper, and Ralph Westfall. *Marketing Research Text and Cases*. Homewood, Ill.: Richard D. Irwin, 1972, pp. 617–38.
- Green, Paul, and Donald Tull. *Research for Marketing Decisions*. Englewood Cliffs, N.J.: Prentice-Hall, 1966, pp. 163–77.
- Martineau, Pierre. *Motivation in Advertising (Motives That Make People Buy)*. New York: McGraw-Hill, 1957.
- Smith, George H. *Motivation Research in Advertising and Marketing*. Westport, Conn.: Greenwood Press, 1971.

Most authorities on the advertising industry agree that the most important quality an ad can have is believability. Can consumers visualize themselves using the product or service? As one advertising executive put it, "All business is done in the human mind."

Do people really need the vast array of products and services advertised? Pat Steel, a veteran advertising executive, answers the question this way: "People don't really need these things—art, music, literature, newspapers, historians, wheels, calendars, philosophy. All people really need is a cave, a piece of meat, and possibly, a fire." Helen Woodward, in *It's an Art,* states that "the best ads aren't the ones about which you say, 'Isn't that clever?' but the ones which make you take out your pocketbook and buy something."

WHAT A COPYWRITER NEEDS

To effectively sell a product or service, a copywriter needs a strong knowledge of the product, a commercial sense, logic, a prolific imagination, a keen selling instinct, good judgment, the ability to write, a sentimental streak, plenty of curiosity, a sense of humor, and a fondness for people.

Perhaps the one element common to the better copywriters is previous sales experience. Advertising is a selling business, and everything in advertising is geared to move the product and please the client.

A certain flair for the English language is a definite help. In the words of Bernice Fitz-Gibbon, another advertising professional, "Nothing else will give a copywriter the same surge of self-confidence that knowing the English language will." Obviously, any copywriter should have (or develop) a deep love for working with words. Unless you intend to sell only a few basic products by mail order, you will need to develop good copywriting skills. The more products you sell, the more copywriting you will be planning and producing.

Mark Twain stressed the importance of words in another way: "A powerful agent is the right word. Whenever we come upon one of these intensely right words in a book or a newspaper, the resulting effect is physical as well as spiritual, and electrically prompt."

If you don't feel confident about working with words, don't let it keep you out of mail order. You can learn how to use words effectively, as surely as you learned how to walk as a child. Advertising writing is a craft, and a craft can be learned.

7

How to Save Money on Advertising

YOUR OWN "IN-HOUSE" AGENCY

If you plan to be in mail order for any length of time, you will save money by setting up your own ad agency. Don't let this worry you. It's not complicated at all. Most publications give ad agencies a 15 percent commission, usually in the form of a discount on all ads placed. Choose a name for your own agency and have some separate letterheads printed; you will save yourself 15 percent. Many people who own and operate a mail-order business place their ads through their own "in-house" agencies.

In starting your business, you would be wise to operate from your home or apartment. You can store your business materials and product stock in a closet, as many small firms do. Go slowly at first and plan your moves in advance. This will save you time and money in the long run.

You will be the one planning and writing the ads to sell your products. And you will choose the mail-order publications in which to run your ads. So you will have done all the work—not some outside ad agency. If you run 50 or more ads in a year, preparing and placing them yourself will amount to considerable savings.

Before I started running my first ads, I chose a name for my own agency and had 1,000 letterheads printed with my agency name and address on them. To avoid confusion, try to pick a name that hasn't been used. Some possibilities are Creative Advertising, Novelty Advertising, or Southern Advertising.

I still do business under my own in-house agency name. I ran a lot of ads during my first year in mail order, so I saved a considerable amount of money. You can do the same. If you ever wish to offer an advertising service, your agency letterheads will come in handy. In addition to my mail-order selling, I did some advertising copy work for several large companies. These companies have since developed into regular clients. I do advertising, public relations, and sales promotion for them on a regular basis.

Most publications will accept the ads you wish to place through your in-house agency without question. I never had any trouble, and my ads have appeared in just about all the leading mail-order magazines. Some publications say they won't accept in-house agency ads, but this is usually said just to keep the recognized advertising agencies content. Such restrictions are seldom actually enforced.

Remember: A mail-order magazine will not give you the 15 percent discount on your ad if you place the ad through your mail-order company. Although your in-house agency is, in reality, only a name on a letterhead, it is necessary for the discount. You might wish to use a different address for your agency, but I used the same address for both my agency and mail-order company, and I never had any trouble.

I also opened a separate checking account at my bank in the name of my in-house agency. I then paid for the ads I ran with checks showing my agency name and address. I see no reason why you can't do the same.

WHAT YOU SHOULD KNOW ABOUT YOUR BUYER

Regardless of the product, service, or other offer you sell by mail, you'll eventually come to realize a vital truth about the world of selling today: Today's buyer is very selective.

Why is this so? Why have consumers become so choosy about what they buy? There are three basic reasons. By understanding these you'll have a better idea of how to motivate prospects into sending you an order.

The buyer of today is hard to please. Most are relatively well-educated, fairly sophisticated in their likes and dislikes, and more selective.

Today's Buyer Is Well-Educated

Is it really true? Is today's buyer all that well-educated? Yes. Most buyers know a good deal about a lot of things. They've learned a great deal just from watching television each evening over a period of years. It's also true that many of today's buyers have either a college education or at least some years of college behind them. Service in the armed forces has added to the overall education of many, and a number of recent studies indicate that the amount of time spent on reading has gone up in several countries.

The fact that the buyers of today are well-educated has broad implications. It means that buyers of the late twentieth century are sharp and will probably grow sharper. It's not just book learning between their ears; prospects are wise to the realities and problems of contemporary life. They know who they want to vote for and why, and what kind of products, services, and offers they're willing to spend money on.

What does all this mean to you, as a mail-order operator trying to interest prospects in your products and offers? It means that your advertising strategy must take the high educational level of your buyers into account if you're going to be consistently effective in getting a share of the business.

Today's Buyer Is Sophisticated

Buyers today are very aware of the value of products and services in general. They're sophisticated about buying. They've learned from both good and bad purchases in the past. They've also been bombarded with media advertisements and commercials, so they've heard or seen literally thousands of commercial plugs and sales pitches. What this all adds up to is a high level of sophistication that comes into play whenever they make buying decisions.

Buyers can be grouped into three categories. To begin with, there's the brainy buyer. This person is often the hard-boiled business type who is rarely, if ever, swayed by emotion. The brainy buyer uses plenty of deduction and logic when making decisions.

Another type of buyer is the emotional person. This type usually gets along well with people, is fond of fancy food, usually dislikes physical labor, and often makes spontaneous choices based on feelings.

A third kind of buyer is simply a combination of the brainy and emotional types. This type wants to both think and feel right about any deal being considered.

Unfortunately, your mail-order ads and direct-mail sales letters can't sort out which prospects fall into which of these categories. But if you run your ads in the leading mail-order publications, you can be sure that large numbers of people from all three groups will be exposed to your ads. So your sales messages should be beamed at all three kinds of buyers. Also, if you send out enough sales letters to the people on good name lists, you'll be communicating with all three categories of buyers.

Today's Buyer Is Selective

People may be fairly quick to spend $5.00, $10.00, or even $20.00 for a given product. But most of them will do some real thinking before deciding to buy a $50.00, $75.00, or higher-priced item. When the economy of a country goes through depressed periods, this naturally has an effect on the buying decisions of most prospects. It makes them more selective.

Although you won't see the prospects who respond to your ads and offers, it's still a good idea to try to keep up with their changing nature. It's entirely possible for a mail-order operator to know the product well and have a strong series of ads or sales letters, but still lack an understanding of the prospects.

You can never know too much about the prospects you're trying to reach and the changes affecting them. You should try to develop a real sense of the pressures and influences being exerted on your prospective buyers.

SOME SOUND ADVICE FOR YOUR SUCCESS

Remember: Prospects and customers are the lifeblood of your mail-order business. There's always more to learn about them and about ways of communicating your sales message to them more effectively.

Andrew Carnegie gave some fine advice on success. He advised those wanting success to "put all your eggs in one basket, and then watch that basket. Men who do that do not often fail."

There's nothing to prevent you from learning more about the prospects and customers you hope will build your business. Why do some buy and others fail to respond to your offers and ads? Why do some seem to understand and react promptly to your mail offers? The answers to such questions can do a lot to increase your sales and profits.

Some wise and forward-thinking mail-order operators include a reply card or return note in the direct mail they send out. They ask prospects to state their reason or reasons for not responding to a particular offer. Naturally, many prospects won't give their reasons, but a number of them do. Such information can be very helpful when planning future offers and direct mailings.

You might consider keeping a continuing diary or observation book in which you write down various notes and other things you learn about prospects and customers. You could call your book *What I've Learned about Selling to Prospects and Customers by Mail.* The idea would be to form the valuable habit of recording the observations and ideas you have gained from dealing with prospects. You might be surprised at how much you can learn by using this method.

So keep in mind the fact that today's buyer is changing. Just being aware of this fact and responding to the knowledge that the prospects you'll be dealing with by mail are generally sophisticated, selective, and smart makes you a better mail-order operator and a more successful one.

MOTIVATING YOUR PROSPECTS TO TAKE ACTION

Having an attractive product or service to offer is vitally important to your success in mail order. But landing the sale is crucial too. Unless you motivate your prospects to take action and send you an order, your products and services won't move. You need a steady flow of orders coming in to keep your business growing.

Can you close enough sales? The answer to this question will determine your degree of success in mail order, regardless of the products or services being sold.

Unlike those who sell to prospects on a face-to-face basis, in mail order you depend on the total effect and pulling power of your ad or direct-mail letter. You don't have the prospect beside you, so you have no chance to answer objections or questions about the offer. Your prospect cannot inspect the product and try it out. the words of your ad or sales letter represent you and your offer. So the overall sales appeal must be strong enough to make your prospects decide to send you an order at once.

A face-to-face salesperson develops a kind of sixth sense by knowing just when to close a sale. Not so in mail order. Your ad or sales letter is your calling card. So every word must count. Your prospects must feel a desire to take action. Your offer must arouse their interest, and your ads must make them buy at once.

Think about the big selling job you're expecting your ad or sales letter to do for you. You're expecting your ad to grab attention quickly, to attract interest in your offer, and to motivate prospects to take immediate action. That's a lot to expect. But the fact that many ads continue to produce excellent results in exactly this way is one of the fascinating aspects of mail order.

Truly effective ads that get results call for action. This appeal can be a direct request—even a command—for the prospect to "buy now," "order today," or "send the coupon at once."

This call for action to buy is often mixed with some special incentive or extra appeal, which makes it harder for the prospect to resist buying. Such incentives may be something offered free or a discount if the prospect buys now. Some kind of free gift is often used as the bait to hook prospects. So try to think of some kind of incentive or bonus you can offer prospects if they buy at once or within a certain time period. Many prospects will take action and send you an order because of their desire to get an extra bonus you've offered them. Everyone likes a surprise; they like to anticipate the nature of a gift.

If your product or service offers any extra bonus tie-in, be sure to let prospects know in your ads and sales letters. You could, of course, spotlight such a bonus incentive in a sales letter. A letter gives a lot of space to work with. A small classified ad limits the number of words you can use, but you can still fit in this extra incentive to buy.

A phrase that has worked well for me, in both ads and sales letters, is this: "Surprise bonus gift with your order." I developed this phrase myself and found that it usually doubled the orders I received.

Millions the world over are looking for bargains today. The same thing will no doubt be true in the year 2000 and beyond. When prospects know they're going to get the product or service they order, plus a free bonus or gift, they're much more motivated to buy. It's just human nature.

So I encourage you to add some kind of basic incentive to your ads and sales letters. You may not be able to do it for every offer, but use it whenever you can. It will definitely increase the number of orders you receive. To be sure that your prospects know about any extras you're offering, bring it out in your ads and near the end of your sales letters. The addition of a P.S. at the end of your sales letter is an excellent way to remind your prospects of any gift or extra bonus you're offering.

To help you decide on an incentive to offer, several possibilities follow. Refer to this list when planning new ads, copy, and offers.

Limited Supply. When your product supply is running low, use phrases like "Order now—while they last." There are lots of prospects who will make a quicker buying decision if they believe that your product supply is about to run out. So keep this incentive in mind. People don't like to miss out on a good opportunity or bargain.

Free Gift. This is simply an offer of a free gift to each prospect who sends you an order. A ball-point pen is a good example, but there are numerous other items that you could use. One of my first products was an informational booklet. I had another shorter booklet on a closely related subject printed at the same time. I used this shorter booklet as a free gift and received many comments on it from satisfied customers.

Whatever you use as a free gift, be sure that it isn't too expensive to obtain. You don't want a free gift incentive to eat up all the profits from your basic offer.

Special Offer or Price Cut. There are other ways to say this same thing, such as "clearance," "markdown," or "half-price," but in all of these the idea you're getting across is that the prospect can get your product or offer at a lower price. The savings appeal is a strong one and is used every day in marketplaces throughout the world.

Free Catalog. This assumes, of course, that your business has developed to the point where it's both wise and practical for you to produce a catalog. The offer of a free catalog is appealing to many prospects. It often works well for items that can be ordered again and again. A catalog increases your chances of making sales, for many of today's catalogs offer quite a variety of items.

Free Guidesheet. This can work well if your basic offer or product is in the informational category. I once tried to sell a guidesheet directly from an ad. Orders were not what I had hoped for, but the guidesheet worked very well later as an incentive gift. I have used guidesheets successfully as free gifts many times.

Here is what I believe would be an excellent idea for either an incentive gift or product item itself. A recent study revealed that the average family now takes 2.8 vacations a year plus an average of 7.6 weekend trips away from home per year.

My idea is a booklet or guidesheet that would provide basic vacation tips and information for families. It could include pointers on house or apartment security when on vacation, information on resorts and hotels, the best times for vacations, things to do on vacation, side trips, and the like.

Used as either a primary product or free incentive gift, I believe prospects would be pleased with such a vacation guide. A booklet of this type would require a lot of research and writing, but it could be planned and written up as a one- or two-page guidesheet in practically no time at all.

Price Rise.   This is a variation on the savings angle. As a mail-order operator, you are free to lower or raise the prices of your products and services as you choose. Just as prospects are motivated to buy when you lower a price, they will also buy before a rise in the price. So for an extra incentive, be sure to let prospects know in your ads and sales letters when the price is about to go up.

Special Benefit.   At times products become especially important to prospects because of some government announcement, national trend, or current timeliness. A good example is a snow and ice scraper. When winter is more severe than usual such items are in greater demand. A special benefit thus serves as an extra incentive to buy a product or service.

Guarantee.   This one has already been cited as an important way to increase the number of orders you receive. It belongs in this list because it remains one of the strongest incentives of them all to buy. Be sure to use it in most of your offers. Set a time limit if you wish—for example, a 10-day, two-week, or 30-day guarantee.

There are other possible incentives such as a free sample, introductory offer, or a prize with every order. But the above list will give you some incentives that are used regularly in mail order. They will help to motivate your prospects to send you an order at once.

I greatly increased the number of orders for a music guide when I offered prospects a free bonus gift. I didn't say exactly what it would be, referring to it only as a "bonus gift." I see no reason why you can't do the same. What your own bonus gift will be is up to you. Even items that don't sell well might be used as gifts or bonus extras to induce prospects to buy from you. You will learn a lot by trying out different incentives.

Never underestimate the importance of curiosity. Prospects may send you an order or a request for more details just out of curiosity. Many will simply want to know what your "bonus gift" is, or what your free sample is like. Curiosity is a powerful motivator. Your basic offer must, of course, be clear and specific, but it's fair to whet a prospect's curiosity with extras. Incentives will increase your business. Use them.

THE TRUTH ABOUT FREE ADS

During my early months in mail order, I ordered several manuals and booklets on how to succeed in the business. In a number of them, I read a pie-in-the-sky description of how to get free ads for any item I sold by mail.

I'd like to warn you about this free ad talk. Free ads are apparently a widespread myth of the industry. The search for them certainly proved to be a complete waste of my time, postage, and effort.

I followed the instructions and tips on how to obtain free ads exactly. I did just as the manuals instructed. In one system for getting free ads, I was directed to send cover letters containing my requests for free ads to 100 leading magazines. I typed all my cover letters and envelopes for the 100 magazines myself, to save the time and expense. I was brand new to mail order, and I believed what the manuals on the business had said about it being entirely possible to get free ads for my product.

I can only say that I learned the hard way. My cover letters and envelopes were sent to 100 publications and were typed neatly and professionally. I used my letterhead. I described the product I was selling and hinted in each letter (as instructed in the manuals) that I expected to be advertising my product in the future and might decide to use their magazine.

The idea behind free ads, as explained in the mail-order instruction manuals I bought, was to let each publication know that, as a mail-order operator, I wished to test the pulling power of their publication. If results proved good, the first free ad they gave me could lead to a good amount of additional paid-for advertising.

Many of the how-to-succeed-in-mail-order manuals painted a rosy picture of how easy it was to get free ads and how everyone and his brother in mail order had gotten their mail-order companies off to a fine start with them. I was warned to be prepared to handle the flood of cash orders I would be receiving after my free ads had been published in these top magazines.

I can sum up the total results of my campaign for free ads in one word: zero. After following the directions exactly and sending my request letters to 100 magazines not one free ad was allowed. I was disgusted. More than that, I was plain mad at the mail-order operators who had sold me the manuals on getting off to a great start in mail order through free ads. I had paid them good money for false information. To this day, these same manuals and booklets are being sold to newcomers to the business.

I learned a lot from my experience, of course. What may sound good on paper may not work at all in actual practice. Maybe some do succeed in getting free ads, but I don't think it's through the use of the so-called systems I read about. I made up my mind then that if I ever wrote a book about mail order, I would tell the truth about the way the industry works and expose the myth of free ads.

I remember thinking, when I first read about free ads, that it seemed hard to believe that a national magazine would give a new mail-order operator a free ad. But, maybe a national magazine would want to lure new mail-order companies into the fold with the bait of a free first ad. If returns were good and the first ad pulled, those mail-order firms would continue to use that magazine with paid ads.

I had a good first product that was already pulling for me in various well-known mail-order publications. And I had followed the suggested steps for getting free ads to the letter. I reasoned that I would surely have gotten free ads, from at least some of the 100 magazines I wrote, if the free ad system really worked. No such luck. None of the 100 publications I wrote to even replied to my letters.

Another variation of the same myth is based on the idea of sending out publicity letters to numerous publications. The goal is again supposed to be a free ad. I know of nobody in the mail-order industry who ever got a free ad in this way.

Some people in mail order claim that it's possible to get a free editorial mention of your product and company name and address in a publication. If so, I'm sure that it's never referred to as a free ad. Public relations consultants are, of course, skilled at getting editorial plugs in various publications. New product information and company press releases are frequently used by a number of editors. However, I personally do not know of anyone who ever got a free ad or editorial mention by using the specific directions outlined in mail-order instruction manuals.

A much sounder way to get an editorial mention or announcement of your new product would be through the proven services of a respected professional public relations agency or consultant. It would cost you a fee, I'm sure, but it might prove to be worth it.

There's nothing to keep you from writing your own product press releases and sending them to a few national publications. Some magazines have a new product department and often a special editor who handles this kind of material.

I once phoned the editor of a popular magazine to ask about free ads. He denied the whole idea of free ads and said that his magazine had never allowed any. He did state that new products were sometimes announced in one section of his magazine. He said that I was welcome to send in some brief information about my product, but that he couldn't guarantee it would be used.

I think the timing of an information release is very important. If your new product information arrives at the right time and the particular publication isn't overloaded with such material, you might well get an editorial mention.

A WARNING

I hope you'll proceed slowly and cautiously in the early months of your business. It's fine to look over various instructional materials on how to build your business. But, as I've tried to indicate in a number of places in this book, you can't believe everything you read.

Of course, you're welcome to contact major magazines in an effort to get them to mention your new product and your company. You may come up with some way to interest a publication in what you have to offer by mail. Publications frequently run an article about a company or a new product that has wide appeal. But I advise you not to use the term "free ads" when communicating with publications. Refer, instead, to product releases and editorial mentions. You can do far better by starting with classified ads that you pay for. In this way you're sure to get results.

I believe that both the good and the bad sides of the mail-order business need to be reported, and I've sought to cover them in this book. There's a lot of misleading information floating around about all phases of the business. The fact that a manual claims to offer information on building your mail-order business is no guarantee that the information in the manual will be correct. What sounds good on paper may not be workable in actual practice at all.

You'll at least be ahead of many other newcomers to mail order from a close reading and study of this book. Before spending any of your money on a so-called system to get "free ads," ask for proof in the form of names and addresses of other mail-order operators who got these free ads. I, myself, have come to believe more than ever that you don't get something for nothing in this world. You pay for what you get in one way or another.

INCREASING YOUR PROFITS
THROUGH ADVERTISING

The key to profits in mail order is to have one product, service, or offer bringing in orders and showing a healthy profit, and then to expand advertising by running ads for this item in more publications.

Let's say, for example, that after some good test results, you run your first ad in the "Window Shopping" mail-order section of *House Beautiful* magazine. The item you're offering is a T-shirt with a motto or word on it. Your ad appears in the January issue of *House Beautiful* and pulls beautifully for you. You receive several hundred orders and realize a handsome profit over and above your original investment.

You're in. You're at that happy point of knowing you've got a salable product that prospects will order. When you reach this point, it's only simple logic to realize that by advertising the T-shirts in other mail-order publications you can bring in a lot more orders. This is exactly how many newcomers to mail order have built their businesses and done exceptionally well.

So in our example, if your ad for T-shirts pleased you with its strong results in *House Beautiful,* your next step to increase profits would be to run the same basic ad in as many other publications as possible.

If you're uncertain that your ad will pull well in other publications and you'd rather expand slowly, you can simply run the ad in four or five more publications. Then if your ad makes a strong showing by bringing in more orders, you can rest assured that you've got a winner. At this point, you can do any one of three things:

1. Continue to expand your advertising slowly by running the ad in four or five more publications each month or so.

2. Grow fast by putting a large amount of your profits into more advertising. Run your ad in 30 or more publications simultaneously.

3. Take the cautious approach. Maintain a steady level of advertising by keeping your ad in the same number of publications. In this way, you can tell how long the ad will continue to pull. It can be very helpful to know how many months your ad will continue to bring in orders. Then you can be more confident before jumping into a lot of publications at once.

Bear in mind, too, that most magazines are published once a month or 12 times a year. If you run your ad in each monthly issue of 20 different publications, this means that your ad will be appearing 240 times. Still another way to increase the total effect of your ad would be to run the same ad twice or more in the same issue. Should you run the same exact ad so many times? Why not, as long as it keeps pulling a healthy number of orders for you. An alternate choice is to run slightly different versions of an ad in the same issue.

One very successful mail-order operator runs a small classified ad for a course on writing short paragraphs for money. His ad is short—only a few lines—so he can easily afford to run the ad in a lot of mail-order publications. I've seen this ad for paragraph writing just about everywhere. The ad must continue to sell because I've seen it for over 20 years in hundreds of publications month after month. This same ad appears three and four times in some issues of leading mail-order publications like *Popular Science, Popular Mechanics, Outdoor Life,* and *Specialty Salesman.*

So when you have a winning ad, stick with it. Don't change it as long as it continues to pull orders or requests. Never change a pulling ad until you're certain that its pulling power has ended.

MAKE YOUR OFFERS SOUND POSSIBLE TO ACHIEVE

Obviously, there must be a huge market still virtually untapped for selling instruction courses, manuals, and systems. There's some sound psychological thinking behind these very successful products. As mentioned earlier, most paragraphs—especially short ones—aren't that hard to write. Many people can see themselves succeeding at writing them—and cashing checks for them. This offer sounds entirely possible to accomplish. Small paragraphs are certainly easier to write than a complete article or story.

So whatever you offer prospects, try to focus on items that are workable and realistic. Don't make your offer too complicated or involved. Most people think in an A-B-C manner; they can understand two or three basic points at a time. You'll lose many customers with highly technical or intricate materials. Keep your products and instruction materials easy to understand and use, and you are likely to make more sales.

I highly recommend that you send requests for free details on a variety of courses, instruction manuals or booklets, money-making offers, and products. Once you receive the sales literature, read it over. You'll quickly see that the best-selling items make it sound "easy to write for pay," "easy to double your income in real estate," and so on. Take your cue from these best-selling offers. Keep your offers easy to understand. Make them sound workable to your prospects. If you can do this, you'll get a lot more orders and make much more money in mail order.

Part III

MARKETING YOUR PRODUCT OR SERVICE

SUCCESS STORY: Joe Sugarman

One of the kings of the mail-order business is Joe Sugarman, who sells high-priced microelectronic products. He uses full-size ads in leading publications and has become one of the richest operators in the mail-order industry.

Sugarman studied electrical engineering at the University of Miami. To help a local restaurant increase its customers, he wrote an ad for the school paper, which proved to be so successful that Sugarman soon found himself helping other local businesses through his own small ad agency.

In the early 1970s, Sugarman raised about $12,000 and began to sell a small calculator that worked on a new circuit. He advertised the calculator in the Wall Street Journal *and in two weeks he counted a $20,000 profit. He used big display ads, and his calculator kept on selling. He later ran ads in many major magazines and in three months he realized a handsome net profit of $500,000. Sugarman hired some employees and opened an office and a warehouse in Northbrook, Illinois. His company now employs about 50 people and has become the top seller of home burglar alarms and digital watches.*

8

Selling Your Product Directly from an Ad

As a newcomer to mail order, your first objective is to get one item pulling orders for you and bringing you a profit. Your next goal will be to gradually add other items to your first proven one. This is the way most successful mail-order business have developed.

In the majority of cases, a new mail-order operator will sell the first product item directly from an ad. This method is one of three main ways of selling your product or service. The other two ways are the inquiry and follow-up method and the direct-mail approach. In ads the asking prices for products and services should be adjusted periodically to reflect inflation.

It's also possible to have others sell your product from a catalog, which you plan, produce, and distribute to prospects. But at this early stage in your business, you shouldn't even consider a catalog. You'll need time and experience before using a catalog. A catalog also requires that you have a number of products or services to offer prospects. At this point, you should think about one or two items at the most, unless you already have some good mail-order experience and knowledge.

CLASSIFIED ADS

You'd be surprised at how many mail-order businesses were started with small classified ads. These ads are set in type by numerous mail-order publications. They bring in orders. The first few words or short opening phrases of the ads are capitalized, in order to grab the reader's eye. Here's an example of an attention-getting opener for a classified ad offering a way to stop smoking:

SAY GOODBYE TO CIGARETTES!
Proven way to stop smoking.
Send $4.00 to (name of company and address)

A classified ad has no illustration or artwork. The ad consists of the best "selling" words (the fewer words the better) that state what the offer is, the price, and the address where the product or service can be obtained.

You might be wondering whether these small ads can really pull in paid orders on a consistent basis. They certainly do just that, providing the copy is right. Classified ads have been pulling orders for many years. Some individual mail-order operators have received as much as $5,000 in orders from their very first ad. But the product or service offer has to be right, at the right price, in the right publication, and advertised at the right time.

SELLING DIRECTLY FROM AN AD

If you decide to sell your first item directly from an ad, be sure that your asking price for the product is not too high. Anything over $7.00 or $8.00 may be too high. You will often see higher prices quoted in ads, but it would be wise to stay on the safe side with your first product.

In your ad try to convey the idea that what you're offering is a bargain. Again, a price of several dollars suggests to a prospect that the offer may be a bargain. This is especially true if the item is something that cannot be found in stores and is not being offered by other mail-order firms.

The following are examples of ads that sound like bargains:

50 Different Foreign Coins, $3.00.
(company address)

Garage Sale Kit. Everything needed for
successful sale. Includes signs, stickers,
tags, and booklet. $1.75. (company address)

Another advantage of low-priced items is the simple way in which the offers can be stated. The first ad states the offer in just four words. This is the type of brevity that saves you money. But if you were trying to sell an investment plan or correspondence course, you would need a lot more copy to describe the item.

If you want to sell your first product straight from an ad, but the item is priced above $5.00, you can still try it out. Some people in mail order disagree with the idea that only low-priced items can be sold from an ad. Although you need more space and words to describe your offer, your ad just might pull enough high-priced orders to return a good profit. But, generally speaking, your chances of a good return will be improved if your offer is priced between $5.00 and $10.00. Some even feel that $5.00 to $7.00 is high enough.

Here is a checklist to help you determine if you should sell an item directly from a classified ad:

1. Is the item low-priced?
2. Does the item sound like a bargain? Can you get this idea across in a few well-chosen words?
3. Is the item something people need? Often repeat items like a printing service, address labels, or office supplies are preferable. But it's more difficult to establish an item that must be ordered again and again.
4. Does your item offer genuine value that will leave your customers satisfied?
5. Would your item interest a lot of prospects? If the offer is too specialized, you would be better off not trying to sell it from an ad.
6. Is your item something different or unusual? This novelty effect might put it over big for you. Ask yourself if there's some way you could give your product or offer this effect.

If you can give a yes answer to the above six questions, you probably have an item or offer that can be sold with some success directly from an ad.

As a further help in deciding whether to sell an item directly from an ad, here are some ads currently being seen in the classified sections of reliable mail-order publications. You might compare an item or offer that you're considering with some of these. Notice the few words used to describe each offer, the idea of a bargain, and the low prices quoted.

Parents: Help Your Child Obey! Booklet, send $1.00. (address)

1,000 Embossed Business Cards $7.35 postpaid. (address)

How Intelligent Are You? Self-scoring test reveals I.Q. in minutes. Only $2.50. Guaranteed. (address)

Exotic Flaming Main Dishes and Desserts! Fifteen easy recipes $2.00 plus s.a.s.e. (address)

European Travel! Terrific tips! Save time, money. $1.50. (address)

Complete Divorce. Marriage laws All 50 States. $2.00. (address)

Learn to Type! Complete information with phonograph record and keyboard makes it real easy. $5.98 complete. (address)

How to Win Contests! Amazing new booklet reveals 15 winning secrets plus suggested form and letters. Satisfaction guaranteed. $2.00 Ppd. (address)

Eight Hamburger Recipes from Around the World. $1.50. (address)

Hangliding. Information package, $1.00. (address)

Genuine Australian Opals. 0.50 carat $6.50. (address)

25 Simple Formulas Can Make You Money—all 25 for $1.00. (address)

"Trap" Yourself to Success! $12.95. (address)

Only the last ad on the list has a high price. Many of these ads sound like bargains and are no doubt pulling orders.

SOME GOOD REASONS FOR USING CLASSIFIED ADS

Here are some of the main advantages of using a small classified ad to introduce and advertise your product or service:

1. Classified ads are a definite bargain. The price per word has risen in recent years, but big established mail-order companies continue to use these little ads because they pay off handsomely in both new orders and names.

2. Classified ads don't require years of advertising knowledge and

experience. They are generally easy to plan, write, and place in mail-order publications. Your skill at writing the copy for them will grow quickly.

3. Many mail-order firms actually got started in the business with these little ads, offering one or two items.

4. A classified ad is a fine way to test a new product idea without spending a lot of money.

5. You can learn the basic advertising appeals—in a do-it-yourself way—through classified ads.

6. Nothing is required for these little ads except the wording you want to use.

7. A classified ad enables you to get your product or service message in the pages of a mass-circulation magazine reaching a million or more people. The larger the circulation, the greater the chance that your ad will be seen by buyers interested in your offer.

8. By using classified ads you can set your own rate of growth.

9. You can quickly increase your profits on an item that's pulling orders for you by running more classified ads in other mail-order publications.

10. Classified ads can also be used to obtain the names of prospective buyers. By offering to send free information on your offer to those who write and request it, you can stock up on new names.

WHERE TO RUN YOUR ADS

A question you'll need to answer many times in your business is where to run the ads for your product or service.

Here is a partial list of the leading mail-order publications. The addresses are not given because of location changes that take place occasionally. Also, some magazines go out of business, and others come along. You will find, however, that most of these magazines and some of the newspapers (especially the tabloids) are very effective publications in which to run your first ads.

Many mail-order professionals continue to use these known mail-order publications for the items they launch. You can find the addresses of these publications in *Writer's Market* (published each year). You can also find most of them in the New York Yellow Pages since most of the names on this list are magazines located in New York City. There are a number of other publications you could also use. But the following are some of the best:

- *Selling Direct* (Atlanta, Georgia)
- *Salesman's Opportunity* (Chicago)
- *Income Opportunities* (New York)
- *House Beautiful* (New York)
- *Flower and Garden* (Kansas City)
- *American Home* (New York)
- *Better Homes and Gardens* (Des Moines, Iowa)
- *Grit* (Williamsport, Pennsylvania)—newspaper
- *Capper's* (Topeka, Kansas)—newspaper
- *Fate* (Highland Park, Illinois)—occult magazine
- *Wall Street Journal* (New York)

The Mechanics-Electronics Group

- *Mechanix Illustrated* (New York)—magazine
- *Popular Mechanics* (New York)—magazine
- *Popular Science Monthly* (New York)
- *Popular Electronics* (New York)
- *Radio Electronics* (New York)
- *Elementary Electronics* (New York)

Outdoor Publications

- *Outdoor Life* (New York)
- *Camping Journal* (New York)—magazine
- *Sports Afield* (New York)
- *Field and Stream* (New York)

Tabloid Newspapers

- *The Star* (New York)
- *National Enquirer* (Lantana, Florida)
- *Globe* (West Palm Beach, Florida)
- *National Examiner* (Rouses Point, New York)

Miscellaneous Publications

- *Popular Photography* (New York)

- *The Workbasket* (Kansas City)
- *Farm Journal* (Philadelphia)
- *Modern Bride* (New York)
- *Audio* (Philadelphia)

These publications will get you off to a good start. In time, you will come to know which magazines or newspapers to use for which kinds of products. The mechanics and electronics magazines, for example, are known to pull well for auto-related products, items with male interest, and various how-to offers.

One of the very first things you should do, when starting your mail-order business, is to look at the mail-order sections of some of these publications. This way you can see for yourself what products and services are being offered. You can find most of these publications in the larger libraries. University libraries usually have many of them. Or you may write directly to the publications requesting sample copies. Address your letters to the Classified Advertising Manager.

A mail-order product may have great ads behind it, but unless they're seen by the right buyers nothing will happen. As obvious as this rule may seem, it ranks at the top of the list of reasons why some products don't sell as well as expected.

Much more research is needed to determine the reasons why people remember one product and forget others. Some of the larger companies are doing something about this. Holiday Inns, according to a key executive, created a broad research-marketing plan, which include such areas as media and motivational research. Detailed studies were done to determine which media is best for a given type of advertising and why.

The logical question that an advertiser is faced with is "Why don't sales go up?" Mail-order operator X comes up with an effective series of ads. They are placed in the right publications. Then why don't sales move up to the expected minimums? The experts say that four out of five new products are doomed from the moment they leave the drawing boards because ads are placed in the wrong magazines and newspapers, or on the wrong radio and television stations. More and better research provides the key to stronger pulling ads.

The point is that you shouldn't get discouraged if your first ads don't pull as many orders as you had hoped. You'll need time to develop stronger copy for your ads. You will be learning about the various mail-order magazines and which ones are best for your particular offer. Perhaps your first product or service offer isn't right or doesn't have enough appeal. The next product may be a different story. You've got to hang in there and experiment a little. Trying out other new offers can be the step that eventually leads to a successful and profitable business.

PLANNING THE COPY FOR YOUR ADS

Copywriting for your mail-order ads will be covered more fully in Chapter 8. Below are some specific pointers on planning your copy—after you have decided where and when to run them. You can refer to this guide when working out your first classified ad.

1. Take a sheet of paper and write down all the benefits and facts about your product or service. Study your list and try to come up with a central selling idea. This might be just a few words or a key phrase. What you want is something fresh—a main selling point about your product. Some examples are

   "The taste that beats the others cold"

   "Things go better with Coke®"

   For a mail-order classified ad, you'll need something short and snappy, and a selling point that sparkles.

2. Create an opening attention-getting line for your ad. This will be your headline, the first words of which are usually capitalized or printed in bold type. David Ogilvy, a highly respected advertising professional, says that "five times as many people read the headline of an ad as the rest of the words." So hit them hard with a good headline.

3. Make every word in your ad count. Give facts that will make a prospect want to buy.

4. Make your ad a me-to-you message—as if you're communicating with only one person.

5. Mention in the ad whether the asking price is postpaid or whether an extra amount is required for postage. Many ads ask for a small amount of money for sending details on an offer. You'll get more replies, however, if such details are offered free.

6. Keep the words of your ad as simple as possible. Study classified ads regularly looking for examples of simplicity. Make it easy for prospects to understand your offer and to send you an order or request for details.

7. Include the price of your offer and your address. Most classified ads end with the address of the company and a key (a system to indicate which ad brought in the orders).

8. Offer a money-back guarantee on anything you sell, for it usually increases the number of orders you receive. Some experienced pros in mail order, however, believe that the word "guaranteed" may be losing some of its power. Many things are guaranteed today and have been for many years. The word may not be as powerful as it used to be.

9. Be aware that a low-priced item ($5.00 or less) will usually take a smaller amount of space and copy than a high-priced item or offer.

10. Make no changes in the copy until orders have fallen off considerably and you're sure that the ad has run out of steam.

11. Try to write copy that appeals to a mass audience.

12. Get someone with a knowledge of advertising to help you if writing the copy for your ads is too troublesome. If you use a recognized advertising agency for help, try to pick one that has had a considerable amount of experience in mail order.

13. Make the promise of your offer as clear and specific as possible.

14. Use attention-getting words in your copy. Some of the most powerful words in classified advertising copy include the following:

    - Free
    - Valuable
    - Amazing
    - Secret
    - Limited Supply
    - Exciting
    - How-to
    - Now
    - Easy
    - Unique
    - Weekly
    - Guaranteed

15. Think of copywriting as the art of seeing a product or service in a fresh way.

16. Present the benefits of your offer in a variety of ways. Look for new and effective ways to describe your product or service. Make every word pull its own weight in your ad. Small classified ads can bring you a steady supply of orders and money, so take the necessary time and effort to plan and write them effectively.

THE IMPORTANCE OF KEYING YOUR ADS

One term that confuses newcomers to mail order is "keying an ad." Briefly stated, a key for an ad means a simple way of identifying orders pulled in by a particular ad, so you can know how many orders each ad has produced. This clearly is important information to have.

You might think of a key for an ad as a code you use to decipher how much business your ads are pulling for you. The truth is that some copy will do better for you than others. So it helps to be able to spot which ads seem to be the winners. Then you'll know which ones to keep running.

The kind of key to use is a decision you must make when you plan and write the copy for your ads. Once you've sent your insertion order to a publication, you usually cannot make any changes in or additions to your ad. This is especially true if a set date for any and all changes has passed. So be sure that each ad you send in has a key. This system is especially helpful when you're running several ads in different mail-order magazines or newspapers at the same time.

There are different ways to key an ad. You can choose which one you like best or even think up your own method of keying. Here are some of the usual types:

1. A key with two parts. One or two letters, for example, are used to indicate the publication. A number follows the letter or letters to show which monthly issue of the publication the ad appeared in. It would look like the following:

    SD-3 (SD stands for *Selling Direct,* and the 3 means the March issue)

    If your ad appeared in the *National Enquirer,* the key would look like this:

    NE-8 (Since the *Enquirer* is a weekly newspaper, the 8 would mean the eighth week.)

2. Another way to key an ad is to use a "Dept. No." in the address you give. In other words, each publication in which you advertise is given a different number. "Dept. PM" would then stand for *Popular Mechanics.* "Dept. HB" would be your code for *House Beautiful.*

3. You can use different booklet, bulletin, or folder numbers. This kind of key usually works well when prospects are writing you to request more details and information on your offer. To use this

HOW TO BECOME a selling writer quick!!! Guide—50¢. Wilbur Enterprises. 2555 Laurel Road, Jacksonville, FL 32201.

CREATE—PROSPER!! How to create songs, toys, stories, articles—new profitable ideas. Guaranteed plan plus creative gift—$8.95; Concepts— 2555 Laurel Road, Jacksonville, FL 32201.

EXPLORE THE FABULOUS Estate and glamorous living of early film star Harold Lloyd! "On-location report. By mail only!! $2.00 ppd. Wilbur Enterprises. 2555 Laurel Road, Jacksonville, FL 32201.

Examples of Successful Classified Ads

method, you would use wording something like the following in your ad: "Request Booklet L" or "Ask for Bulletin S."

4. You can use different post office box numbers, with each number standing for a different publication. This might present problems, however, unless you live in a small town and can make arrangements with the postmaster to use this system. You will probably need an okay to do it, unless you want to actually rent out a number of different boxes.

5. After the address in your ad, you could use "Studio A" or "Studio 1" using any letter or number you like.

6. You could use various code names to stand for different offers or products and publications in which they appear. But with a growing variety of offers or products and services, this could easily become very complicated. Remember: As your business grows, you will want the easiest method for keeping up with the results of your ads.

You might come up with your own ideas about how to key the ads you run. Try to use a simple system that allows for ample growth of the number of ads you run and offers you introduce.

When you're running only one or two ads, you obviously don't have much need for a key, but if you intend to keep advertising in a growing number of mail-order publications, a standard key for your ads will prove to be very helpful.

As the orders and requests for details come in, you can quickly determine which ads are bringing in the best business and the most orders. You'll also be able to spot the ads doing poorly and replace them with something else.

A good thing about using letters and numbers in your key is the fact that they allow more advertising. If you number 1 to 50 or use the letters

A–Z, you will have a system that can be used to identify many different publications.

One of the chief beauties of keying is that it lets you test new ads in various publications. With your key you can be certain which copy works best and in what publications. So key your ads. You'll be glad you did when you're advertising several different items in a dozen or more mail-order publications.

A WORD ABOUT TESTING ADS

Testing is invaluable in the mail-order business. It makes it possible for you to separate the winning ads—the order producers—from the losers. You'd be surprised how many newcomers to mail order have run a few ads, being disappointed at the results, and thrown in the towel.

Let's face it: Unless you're a born advertising genius with a natural feel for the art of motivating prospects to take action, you're going to have to be content—like most others—to grow slowly over a period of time. It's very possible to get rich quick in mail order, but you would be wiser to aim at slow but steady growth.

So, if your first few ads prove to be duds, don't let it throw you. Don't be stampeded out of what could eventually become a most lucrative business for you.

Testing new ads, new copy ideas, and new offers can be the one step that insures your continued success in mail order. It teaches you what will and won't work.

Mail-order publications will charge so much per word. This amount is usually around $10.00 or more per word, depending on the publication and its reputation for getting results for mail-order companies. When you're spending several dollars a word, it's critical to have some advance idea of the results you'll get before running that ad in numerous other publications.

Here are some helpful rules to follow when testing an ad:

1. You can't be sure if you have a winning product or offer until test results prove it.

2. Remember: Your product or offer might be good, but the copy you're using to sell it might be wrong or weak. So test the offer and the copy.

3. One quick way to test is to run your ad in a newspaper. Although most of them are not known as very reliable mail-order pullers, newspapers bring quicker results than monthly magazines. A number of mail-order professionals test in the *New York Times*. Sunday magazine sections published by various newspapers are a good place to test. Results come in fairly quickly.

4. If the results of any test are poor, you may not have to scrap the item or project. Maybe you can redo it. Rewrite the copy, or improve the offer itself. After rewriting your ad or improving the basic offer in one or more ways, you might get much better results on the next test.

5. When results are poor, and few orders or replies are received, it could mean that the root of your trouble lies in the product or offer itself.

6. A good way to test copy is to run different ads on the same offer in the same publication. Then you can see which copy does the best.

7. Remember that you can test the different classifications within a publication (the headings under which your ad appears). You can run one ad under "business opportunities," another in the "money-making opportunity" section, another in the "do-it-yourself" category, and so on. Generally speaking, one of the best places to run your ad is under the "business opportunities" heading. It has a reputation for pulling well. But ask yourself what heading would logically bring the best results for your offer. Then try it.

8. One reason for poor test results may be the fact that too many other mail-order firms are offering the same item or something very similar to it. If too many other mail-order operators are selling your offer, your orders or replies are going to be cut drastically.

9. If you can obtain a well-qualified list of prospects with a known interest in your item or offer, you might try a direct mailing. Direct mail is also a good way to keep your product or offer private for a while, until you can evaluate the reaction to it.

10. Try to avoid testing in the wrong publications. Study the mail-order sections of some of the publications already named. This

will give you an up-to-date knowledge of the kinds of offers and products being advertised in each publication. If you can afford it, test in the better mail-order publications. As mentioned before, however, tests in some newspapers and Sunday magazine sections bring quick results.

11.   Choose the best issue in which to test a particular ad or offer. Generally speaking, the September, November, and January issues of leading mail-order publications are the three best pulling ones. The September and January issues are especially good. Some product items and offers, however, can be advertised with good results in any month. It depends on what you're offering. The mail-order business usually falls off in the summertime, but it picks up again in the fall. January is usually a very strong pulling month for all kinds of offers.

12.   A strong and attractive headline can make a real difference in the test of an ad. Experiment with new headlines when you test. Sometimes a better headline can double your replies.

13.   The right list of names in a direct-mail test can mean the difference between success and failure.

14.   You can test different prices for your products and offers. Watch the price you quote carefully. If it's higher than other mail-order dealers are asking for similar items, it will cost you a lot of business. An offer may pull much better when the price is either raised or lowered. A higher price is sometimes identified with better quality. Test to find out what price works the best. Round dollar prices are usually best for lower-priced items.

15.   If the results of a second test of an offer are poor, you should probably drop that item and try something else. But, if you still have faith in it, try to improve the offer or the ad. Then run a few more tests.

DETERMINING THE COST OF YOUR CLASSIFIED ADS

How much money does it take to advertise? The answer depends on where you run your ads and how often you advertise.

You are charged a set rate for each word in a classified ad. At this writing, the rate for an ad in *Popular Science* (a strong mail-order magazine) is $11.80 per word. By the time you read this, the rate charged could be even higher. A 20-word ad in *Popular Science* could cost you $236.00.

The total bill for your ad will be higher if you choose to have the headline of your *Popular Science* ad appear in boldface type with all capital letters. Any additional words you use over 20 would be extra.

But look at what you would get for a 20-word ad in *Popular Science*. Circulation is large—currently 1,800,000. This should mean a good response to your ad. Close to two million people will see the magazine. You can't count on that many seeing your own ad, of course, but the higher the circulation in a reliable mail-order publication, the better the chances that your ad will pull well.

Remember: You pay for the total number of words in a classified ad. Everything in the ad counts. Single numbers, initials, abbreviations, or groups of figures all count as one word each. Most publications count the zip code used in your company address as one word. A few will let you use your zip code free of charge.

To give you an example of how the word count and cost are figured, here is a classified ad that has always done well for me whenever I've run it:

HOW TO BECOME A SELLING ARTICLE WRITER FAST!
Guide sheet $1.00. Wilbur Enterprises, 203 N. 10th Street, Murray, Kentucky 42071.

Most publications count the above ad as 20 words. If I ran it in *Popular Science* today, it would cost me $236.00. I was teaching in a college in Kentucky when I ran this ad for the first several times.

Notice that by omitting the word "street," in the above ad, one word could be saved. Leave out "street," "avenue," or "drive," whenever you can. It will save you money on your ads. Most mail is delivered safely without these extra words in the address. Most mail is delivered safely without these extra words in the address.

Here are some more examples of correct word count:

Fred E. Smith	(counts as three words)
P.O. Box 7	(counts as three words)
U.S.A.	(counts as one word)
South Bend	(counts as two words)
1979–1980	(counts as two words)

If you should be incorrect on the exact word count and charge for your ad, the classified advertising department of the magazine you deal with will let you know what additional amount you owe. But in most cases, you'll be able to figure the exact cost of your ads.

Just to give you an idea of relative costs, the current rate for a display ad in *Popular Science* is $655.00 for an inch of space. Even *Popular Science,* itself, states in some of its advertising aimed at mail-order advertisers that "dollar for dollar, classified ads are more profitable than big display ads." So it's probably best to stick with classified ads until your business has grown and you believe display ads are justified.

If the *Popular Science* rate of $11.80 per word is too high for you, there are other good mail-order publications that you can use at lower rates. *Popular Mechanics* is a strong pulling choice. Its current rate is $10.20 per word—$1.60 lower than *Popular Science. Popular Mechanics* will set the first word of your ad in boldface at no extra charge. And the use of your zip code is free too. So a 20-word ad in *Popular Mechanics* would cost you just $204.00, which is $32.00 less than the same ad run in *Popular Science.*

The best way to plan and determine the cost of your classified ad is to write to the publications you're thinking about using. Ask them to send you information about their classified rates. They'll be happy to send you a rate card and full details about their circulation, service to mail-order companies, and pulling power. Advertising is their business, and they want your patronage.

Try to form the habit of planning your ads well in advance. Most mail-order publications require that your classified ad copy be sent to them with full payment by a certain deadline date for each issue. Say, for example, that you wish to run a classified ad in the May issue of *Popular Mechanics.* The copy for your ad, just as you want it to appear, must be received by the magazine by March 10 in order to be published in the May issue. By writing to each publication and requesting full advertising details, you can obtain specific deadline information for each issue and be certain to have your ad in on time.

When writing to publications for information and advertising rates, address your letter as in the following example:

Classified Advertising Manager
Popular Mechanics Magazine
224 West 57th Street
New York, New York 10019

Publications sometimes move so be sure that you use the current address. Most large libraries have up-to-date issues, so you can check the current address, if in doubt.

After you have written to the publications for the first time, you'll have the names of the classified advertising managers, and can address them personally from then on. It's a good idea to keep all advertising rate information in a special file, or, if you wish, you could set up a separate file for each mail-order publication in which you expect to be advertising.

Most mail-order publications require a minimum insertion. By this they mean that they will not accept any ad with less than a certain number of words. The minimum number of words required at *Popular Mechanics* and at most other publications is 10. This is no problem. When you think about it, it's almost impossible to state what your offer is and give your company name and address in fewer than 10 words. Even when you try to scrimp on words to save money it's hard to write an effective ad in less than 25 words.

I've run ads with fewer words—10 in some cases—but they didn't pull nearly as well as those with more. It's possible to get good results from a brief ad if you're advertising a catalog or similar item. Experiment to see what number of words works best for you.

ESTABLISHING CREDIT FOR ADS

After you've run a number of ads in the same publication, you'll find it possible to establish credit. When a magazine has seen that you've paid for your previous ads in advance and that you appear to be a reliable and regular customer, they may allow you credit on future ads.

With credit you can pay for your ads after cash orders have started to come in. This can be a big help because it lets you run many ads without having to pay in advance for them. In this way, you can eventually have many ads appearing in a variety of mail-order publications.

Most publications will send you a complimentary copy of the issue in which your ad appears. This is proof that your ad was published.

Many mail-order publications also offer what is known as a "frequency discount." If you run more than one ad in the same magazine, you can usually get a discount on the total charge as a reward or inducement to advertise in that publication. Three or four ads run in succeeding issues can save you money. Ask about this when you contact various mail-order magazines.

SENDING IN YOUR AD INSERTION ORDERS

Once you've planned your ad and figured the cost, you're ready to submit your copy to the publications you have selected.

An insertion order is your instruction to a publication to run an ad in one issue. There are three basic ways you can send in your order.

First, fill in the classified advertising order form provided by the magazine. When you first write to publications for their advertising rates, they will send you a special form for sending in your ad copy.

Beginning with the 15th word or so, many publications will even figure the cost for you in advance. You have only to type in the words of your ad exactly as you want them to be published, and enclose your check or money order. Many publications will let you charge the cost of your ad.

Be sure that your company name and address are on the form before mailing it. If at all possible, type in each word of your ad neatly. Typing makes your copy easier to read. You want every word to be clear, so there will be no mistakes in the final published ad.

A second way to send in your order to run an ad is to draw up your own special form to use whenever you run new ads. Have enough copies of your form printed so you won't run out. A hundred or so would be a good initial supply, unless you expect to be doing a great deal of advertising.

Use your mail-order company letterhead (or, if you have one, your in-house ad agency letterhead) for this order form. Near the top—just beneath your company name—leave some space for the name and address of the publication you're sending your order to (see Figure 8-1).

You can arrange the information on the form in any way you wish, but it's a good idea to include most of the divisions shown on the sample form. A classified advertising manager or assistant can tell from a glance what you're advertising, who you are, the heading you want your ad under, the issue you want it in, the number of words in the ad, and the exact copy for the ad.

Near the bottom of your form be sure to have the following words: Total Amount Enclosed for This Ad. After you've filled in the information for each ad you order, the last thing you do is type in the amount required for the ad, as you have figured it. Then simply enclose a check or money order when you send the form.

By completing one of your own special forms for each ad insertion order you send to a publication, you'll be making it very clear what you

---

THE JOHN BROWN COMPANY
1716 Bluford Street
Phillipsburg, N.J. 08865
(201) 766-9453

(Insert name and address of publication)

Product Advertised: (state nature of product—booklet, service, etc.) _____

Heading: (Business Opportunities, Do-It-Yourself, or other category) _____

Publication in Which Ad Is to Appear: (name of publication) _____

Date Ad Is to Appear: (issue date or month ad will appear) _____

Number of Times Ad Is to Be Run: (one or more times) _____

Key: (type in your code for the ad) _____

Number of Words in Ad: (total number of words) _____

Copy for Ad: (leave enough space so that all the words of your ad can be

neatly typed) _____

_____

Rate Per Word: (insert the rate per word charged by the publication) _____

Total Amount Enclosed for This Ad: _____

15 Percent Agency Commission
(include if you are using your ad agency letterhead)

Figure 8-1

want done. Keep a copy for your own records. A publication might lose your order form or even your payment for an ad. You can also refer back to the copy when reviewing ads you've run or checking copy you've used.

A third way to send in your ad instructions is to type a short business letter to the classified advertising manager. State the issue you want your ad to appear in and the heading you want it under. The earlier you send in your insertion order, the more likely you'll be to get the heading you want.

After a paragraph or two of instructions, simply type the words of your ad. Enclose payment for the ad with your letter, unless you're charging it. Be sure to use your company letterhead for any letter ordering an ad. Also, be sure to type such letters—it's far more businesslike. In fact, try to type all communications to a publication, so they'll be sure to understand what you want.

YOUR OWN ADVERTISING AGENCY ORDER FORM

Many mail-order companies that set up their own in-house ad agencies (see Chapter 7) use the ad order form like the one shown in Figure 8-1. If you order ads through your own ad agency, you'll want to include a division on your order form (near the bottom of the page) reading like this: "15 Percent Agency Commission." Any ads you order through your own ad agency will then be allowed a 15 percent commission. This means that you can subtract 15 percent from the total cost of your ad.

If you would rather not figure this commission discount yourself, the publication will be glad to do it for you. But be sure you mention this 15 percent agency commission somewhere on your order form if you're using your own legitimate ad agency.

DISPLAY ADS

Until you've gained some experience running your company, it would be best to rely on classified ads to bring in the orders or inquiries you receive. It's good preparation, however, to start learning about display ads from the beginning. Because they are much larger than classified ads—and certainly more attractive—display ads bring in a lot more orders and larger profits. They can expand your business to the point where literally millions of people are seeing the ads for your products and services.

Many display ads have a picture or illustration of the product being offered, so prospects can actually see what they will receive for their money. The ads in the "Window Shopping" section of *House Beautiful* are one-twelfth-page ads. A picture of the advertised product appears in every one of these "Window Shopping" ads. They pull orders quite well. A one-twelfth-page ad in this popular mail-order section would cost you $2,525. (This price is subject to change.)

House Beautiful, through its popular "Window Shopping" section, has run more mail-order ads than virtually any other magazine for over 35 years. A display ad in this excellent publication will bring you fine results and possibly even mailbags crammed with orders. Assuming you have a sound product or service to offer and your ad is well planned, your first display ad in *House Beautiful* might go a long way toward launching your business.

When you feel confident that you have a strong product, and have some classified experience behind you, you might think seriously about trying a display ad in *House Beautiful*. The "Window Shopping" staff at *House Beautiful* consists of real pros, and they'll be glad to help you with your first ad.

When preparing display ads, some mail-order firms hire the services of a recognized mail-order advertising agency. But this could be expensive. *House Beautiful* will accept an ad you prepare yourself, provided that you submit certain things along with it. To run your display ad the magazine would need the following items:

1. Photograph—You would of course need to have a good quality photo of your product made. If you're selling on a drop-ship basis, getting your product from a supplier, the company that manufactures the product may be willing to give you some photographs. You could then send one of these to *House Beautiful*.

2. The copy for your display ad—The copy would include your headline phrase, all the words of your ad stating the offer, and your company name and address. Each line of copy should consist of 30 to 32 characters (counting spaces). Be sure to include whether the price you are asking is postpaid or not. Your copy must be as clear as possible. Make it easy for prospects to understand your offer so they can order from you.

Terrific Trio of Stacking Tables

Sturdily-crafted, already-assembled, nest of three tables with crystal glass tops in metal bamboo styling fill many decorative needs. Use them together or separately for extra occasional tables. Overall 3 tables: 23Lx16Wx21"H, 19Lx13Wx19"H, 15Lx-10Wx17"H. Order in either rich KOCH brass plate (B) or Contemporary nickel plate (N). SBNT-1, $159.50. Shipped prepaid upon receipt of check.

St. Nicholas Boutiques
SANTA CLAUS, INDIANA   47579

A sample layout and an actual ad that appeared in *House Beautiful's* "Window Shopping" section. A good illustration and clear, concise copy make for an effective ad.

3. Layout—This is simply a sketch of the way your ad will look. The size of your ad can be proportioned according to the one-twelfth-unit size of the "Window Shopping" ads. Half of the space will be for your photograph. The rest will be for copy. Your headline can be written in pencil, and lines can be used to denote the main body of your ad. You can get a good idea of how your ad will look by using some of the ads in *House Beautiful* as a guide. You should make it a regular habit to look over the pages in each "Window Shopping" section.

Remember: It may be better in some cases to have a display ad prepared by an advertising agency (one that understands mail order). But it's entirely possible for you to plan your own ad. The copy and layout aren't that hard to do. Getting a photograph of your product may be the most difficult part of all.

If you can see yourself in mail order for the long haul and you plan to be doing display ads sooner or later anyway, there's a lot to be said for learning how to send magazines what they need to run your ads. Once you understand the process and requirements, you're free to run your display ads in any of the leading mail-order publications.

How soon you work your way up to display ads depends on how quickly you learn the basics of mail order, how good a product or service you have, and whether you can afford the cost. These ads are, of course, much more expensive.

For most newcomers to mail order, I would advise you to run a number of small classified ads first. This will develop your overall confidence and teach you the mail-order fundamentals. Many who come into mail order wait six months to a year or longer before running a display ad. Some never do and are content to stick with classifieds and direct mail.

Whatever your preference, don't rule out display ads as a future possibility. You might eventually do very well with them. It's worth a try when you're ready. The profits can prove to be staggering.

A word of caution is in order at this point. Good photographs will help the total effect of your display ads, but the *copy* of your ad is more important. Remember the advice of advertising genius Claude Hopkins: "The purpose of advertising is not to entertain or be clever; the major purpose of an ad is to sell the product or service."

Will it sell? This is the question to ask again and again. What good is a beautiful ad if it doesn't sell? You're out the cost of the ad—and it might be a hefty amount—so what you want is a display ad that will pull in orders.

Ask yourself if a product idea will sell, will a given headline sell, will the body copy of your ad sell, will the price sell. No ingredient of your ad can be overlooked. Beautiful girls alone won't sell the product. And you want to sell your product or offer—not entertain prospects.

Keep the layouts for your ads simple and sensible. If they are too complicated and confusing, your prospects may be lost. You want your prospects to become intrigued by the copy of your ad. So make them as readable as possible.

Some mail-order firms use both small classified ads and much larger display ads to sell their products and services. You might wish to use both some day, as your business develops and grows.

9

Let's Write a Classified Ad

Sharpen your pencil and get out some paper. Make yourself comfortable, but keep your thinking cap on. You're about to write a classified ad. I'll be your guide as we create one together, starting from just a headline.

This could be one of the most valuable chapters in the entire book. You're going to discover how much fun there is in creating a classified ad. But finding the best way to sell a product or offer is also a real challenge.

Creatively speaking, it's stimulating to work up an attractive classified ad. But remember that what you want is not to entertain the prospect or to show how clever you are. Your only goal must be to choose and use the strongest selling words. You want words that will make prospects send you an order at once.

COPYWRITING PRINCIPLES

1. Appeal to your prospects' curiosity in your ad, for it is a strong human incentive.
2. Realize that people want bargains, but they do not want cheapness.
3. Learn some principles of psychology.
4. Offer identical products in different ways.
5. Be aware of the drives, emotions, and attitudes of consumers.
6. Know that consumers don't always think or act as they say they do.

7. Realize that writing ads is a craft that can be learned through practice.
8. Write copy that is easy to read.
9. Concentrate on one main theme.
10. Use emotional appeals in your copy.
11. Employ the four steps of effective copy—attention, interest, communication, and action.
12. Make your ad understandable.
13. Put a time limit on your offer.
14. Use copy phrases that stimulate action ("Free details").
15. In small classified ads, concentrate on facts. (You don't have room to persuade.)
16. Know your product inside and out before you write the copy.
17. Keep good copy ideas flowing.

CHOOSE A MAGNETIC HEADLINE

The following true story shows that great ideas for headlines can be found anywhere and everywhere.

I know a man named Leroy who has a real talent for repairing shoes. He now owns his own store, after working for others for years. He's a friend of mine and has kept many pairs of my shoes in top condition.

With the prices of good shoes now running over $50.00 a pair, I'm glad I know this skilled shoe man. I resent having to pay $75.00 or $100.00 for the same basic shoe I bought for $35.00 or $45.00 just a few years ago.

In gratitude to Leroy, I decided to try to come up with an ad idea he might use to increase his business. I knew that many people would be delighted with his service once they knew about it.

So I started trying to think up an attractive headline for an ad that Leroy could run in the local paper or even use on a sign in his store window. Here is the headline I created:

Leroy Keeps You Walkin' Happy!!

I walked into Leroy's store one day and hit him with this headline. He was delighted.

"That says it all about what I do for a living—about my business."

"Right. You've kept me walkin' happy now for several years, Leroy. And I'm grateful. So are my feet for that matter."

"That's the kind of line I could use just about anywhere."

Leroy thanked me. And I left his store that day glad that I could show my appreciation for his good service.

My reason for telling you this little story is that it shows the appeal of a strong headline. "Leroy Keeps You Walkin' Happy" could be the start of an effective ad. It would also make an attractive billboard.

Here are some brief pointers about headlines in general. Try to remember them whenever you're looking for a strong opening line.

1. A catchy headline is memorable.
2. The best headlines are usually short. Avoid too many words in the opening line.
3. Prospects want to know what a product will do for them. Often a headline can effectively sum up the benefit to the customer.

Now let's assume, just for example, that you've developed a booklet to sell by mail. It's an $8.95 booklet that would have strong appeal for women looking for an executive position and for other women seeking to reenter the job market. You wish to sell the booklet directly from an ad. With such a booklet as your product, how would you write a classified ad to sell it?

This is your first assignment. What would you use as a headline? We're going to start and complete an ad for this booklet. Take some time now to think about it, then jot down any ideas that come to mind.

TRY TO AROUSE INTEREST WITH A FEW WORDS

If your objective is to get prospects to request more details, you can often do so with a few words. If your goal is to sell something directly from the ad, it will take more words.

To stimulate your thinking, here are some examples of mail-order headlines. They are taken from current classified ads:

- Identification Card Sales Kit!
- How to Borrow Up to $25,000 Without Interest!

- Fastest, Easiest Piano Course in History!
- Start Used Car Brokerage Business!
- How to Start a Resume Writing Business in Your Spare Time!
- Build $3,000 Foam Plastic Home in One Week!
- Mail-order Millionaire Helps Beginners Make $500 Weekly!
- Free Report: "Executive Type Business"
- New Luxury Car Without Cost!
- Get Rich Using Legal Rip-offs!
- $1,000 Monthly as Publisher's Agent!

Now let's compare headlines for the booklet geared for those women who are looking for an executive position. I hope you came up with a strong line that opens your ad, commands attention, and offers your prospects the promise of value for their money. Here are several headlines I came up with and believe would be strong openers:

Women—How to Land that Executive Job!
Land an Executive Job—Whatever Your Age!
Wealth and Status Can Be Yours Too!

Remember: Your goal in writing a headline is to get across the *promise* of what you're offering as quickly as possible. Prospects want to know what's in it for them—what it will do for them. How does your own headline compare with the three suggested above? Maybe you did better than you think.

Do you believe my own three headlines would grab a woman's attention as she scanned a mail-order classified ad section? Certainly those women who are interested in a career—and there are millions of them—would want to read beyond these headlines to find out more about the offer.

Ask yourself if your own headlines would grab the attention of such women and make them want to know more about your offer. You may have come up with several strong headlines for the booklet. If so, try to choose the one you feel would do the best selling job. You could, of course, run several ads with different headlines for the booklet. But, if you were just trying one ad at first, which of your headlines would you select?

When some of the ads you run don't bring the results you want, you might try switching the headline. Sometimes a change in the headline can improve the pulling performance of an ad.

The next step in writing our ad for the booklet is to describe the product. Tell your prospects what the product will do for them. The headline of our ad has implied the promise of the product. So now make the nature of the product clear. Is it a course, a device, a service, a novelty item, or what?

The second line in our ad might be something like this:

New booklet tells how.

A variation of this second line could be as follows:

Proven plan reveals system.

If you used "proven plan," it wouldn't make it as clear to prospects that the product being offered is a booklet. So it would be wiser to substitute the word "booklet" in place of "plan."

Now we have two lines for our booklet ad. Using the second headline (of the three), these lines are:

Land an Executive Job—Whatever Your Age!
New booklet tells how.

The price of the product or offer usually comes next, along with some type of guarantee. There are several ways this could be stated. Here are some of them:

Only $8.95—guaranteed!

Rush $8.95 (guaranteed) cash or money order to

$8.95—one-month guarantee!

If you wish to have a time limit on a guarantee, you might want to state it in the ad, like the third line above does. If the guarantee is 10 days or two weeks, you should say so.

I'll bet you can guess what comes next in our ad. That's right! A call for desired action. Without an appeal to prospects to take action, by sending you an order at once, an ad would be stripped of one of its essential elements. Make it a definite rule from the start to always appeal for immediate action.

This action appeal in our ad could be any of the following lines:

Order today!! Sterling Enterprises, (key and address of company)

Write: Morrison Company, (key and address)

Act Now!! (company name, address, and key)

Now lets put all of these lines together to make our total booklet ad:

Land an Executive Job—Whatever Your Age! New booklet tells how.
Only $8.95—guaranteed! Order today!! Sterling Enterprises, 789 Oak,
Dept. PS4, Miami, Florida 39871.

There's our complete ad for the booklet. PS4 stands for the April
issue (4 meaning the fourth month) of *Popular Science* magazine.

Not bad. Who knows? The above ad might just be a winner. It has
some appeal and all the ingredients for pulling orders. The total number
of words is 25 (24 if the zip code is allowed free. Notice the exclamation
marks in the ad. Use them in your ads, for they give an added effect to the
total ad and make it longer when published. The use of "street" or
"avenue" was omitted in order to save one word.

Now let's do another ad for this same product. But this time we'll use
a different headline, description, and appeal:

Wealth and Status Can Be Yours Too! Proven booklet reveals system.
Rush $8.95 (guaranteed) cash or money order to: Sterling Enterprises,
789 Oak, Division SS1, Chicago, Illinois 60601.

This last ad runs a few more words—a total of 27, not counting the
zip code. By cutting the words "cash or money order," you could save
four words and reduce the cost of the ad. This would make a total of 23
words. But you might want to include "cash or money order" in your ad.
The decision is yours. You could save another word, by using just one
word for your company instead of two.

WRITING ADS TO PULL INQUIRIES

Many experienced mail-order operators have discovered that selling products priced over $10.00 directly from an ad may not bring the desired
results. The sales of our booklet on landing an executive job might be

higher if we ran some classified ads meant to bring in requests for details rather than cash orders.

If you choose this route, what would some inquiry and follow-up ads be like? Here are a few examples:

Women—How to Land that Executive Job! Free information. Vista-1, 203 Oakdale, Dallas, Texas 78431.

Not counting the zip code, the above ad runs only 14 words. Notice how one word—"vista"—is used. "Vista" could be used here as a key to stand for this particular booklet being offered. The number one after "vista" could stand for the publication in which you're advertising.

Let's try another inquiry and follow-up ad and see if we could make it even shorter:

Women—Land that Executive Job!! Free details. Success-PM 899 Willett, Boston, Mass. 01237.

The ad comes to only 13 words or 14 if you count the zip code. Again, the word "success" could be the code key for the booklet being sold. The letters PM mean that the ad was run in *Popular Mechanics*. If additional ads were run, a number after the letters could indicate which issue was used.

It's perfectly alright for you to try selling a product both directly from an ad and also by the inquiry and follow-up method. Once you learn which selling method pulls the best, you can stick with that choice. Some products priced over $10.00 sell fairly well directly from an ad. You'll have to test specific products and prices. As a general rule, however, items sold directly from an ad will do better if kept under $10.00.

The point is to not get discouraged if a product you try selling directly from an ad does poorly. If the price you're asking is over $10.00, you might just get prospects to send you requests for details by running small ads like the above and following up with sales literature. Of course, you would then need a sales letter to send back to the prospects to persuade them to send you an order.

It's a good idea to actually write several different ads for each product or offer that you plan to advertise. You'll gain some excellent experience, and your chances of coming up with a strong ad will be improved.

Never believe that any particular ad you write is the best you can do. The more ads you create, the better you'll become at it. Copywriting is a developed skill; it improves with time and practice.

By now, you no doubt realize that small classified ads require a short but punchy style. What you're trying to communicate are the basic facts about your product or offer, so a prospect can quickly decide to send you either an order or a request for more details.

DON'T UNDERESTIMATE THE POWER OF CURIOSITY

Curiosity may have killed the cat, but it does human beings a world of good. Stimulate the curiosity of your prospects through the ads you run, and your future in mail order will be successful and profitable.

"Curiosity is, in great and generous minds, the first passion and the last," said Samuel Johnson. For one thing, people in general, and prospects in particular, are more alive when they're curious. This desire to know more about a variety of things is very important.

Curiosity can be an enormous help to you in the writing of classified ads or any other form of advertising. Start forming the habit now of being curious about which selling approaches to use, which headlines may pull the strongest, which prices for your offers are the right ones, which publications are best suited to your products. The answers can mean more money in your bank account.

Curiosity once led me to visit one of the most awesome and historical battlefields of the Civil War: Shiloh National Park. I became fascinated with the place and read more about the battle fought there. In time, I found that I wanted to return again and again to Shiloh, to stand beside the Bloody Pond, to gaze at the cannons now standing silent in the fields, to walk the River Road where Grant walked and planned his military strategy, and to see again the trenches where Northern and Southern soldiers were buried together.

As a result of my visits to the battlefield and my thoughts about what happened I wrote a song. My song, "Shiloh," was recorded and released nationally, receiving strong reaction and comment from key radio market areas. The song brought me mail from just about everywhere.

Remember: Curiosity is often the reason why many prospects will send you an order for your product or a request for additional information. Strive to stimulate curiosity with your ads, and it will pay off for you in more sales and inquiries about your offers.

As an example of using curiosity in a classified ad, I once offered a booklet on building a career in the world of music. Since my asking price for the booklet was $9.95, I decided that it would be best to advertise for inquiries. I worked out a two-page sales letter and had a good supply of copies printed.

I was then ready for my ad to appear. Here is the ad as it appeared in many leading mail-order publications. Notice the element of curiosity in the headline:

> **Secret Plan** Puts You in the Music Business! Free information. Write today!! (my company name, key, and address)

The ad brought in hundreds of requests for more details. I sent a sales letter to each prospect telling more about the booklet. After the sales letter was received by the prospects, I began to receive orders. The ad brought me a handsome profit whenever I ran it. I still offer the booklet today, and the above ad never fails to bring in a large number of inquiries.

Naturally, many of those who wrote to me for more details responded out of curiosity. Look again at the headline of the ad, especially the first two words, "Secret Plan." Let me assure you that one of the most powerful selling words in mail order is the word "secret." There's an almost magical quality to it. Use the word "secret" in your own ad copy whenever you can, if it fits the nature of your product or offer.

I told the truth in my ad. The booklet I offered was indeed a secret plan that would enable the buyer of the booklet to actually get into the music business and build a successful career. I still receive mail today from satisfied customers who bought my career booklet. I'm sure that some of them used the information in the booklet to get into the fascinating music industry. But it was the words "secret plan" that first attracted many prospects to send me a request for free details.

So, if and when you develop some type of informational booklet to offer by mail, look for words and phrases to use in your copy that will appeal to a prospect's curiosity. It's true, of course, that a request for more details may not mean a sale. You will also need a sales letter to motivate prospects to send you an order (see Chapter 12).

You may be wondering if I could have sold my music booklet directly from an ad. Because my asking price as $9.95 (postage paid), I reasoned correctly that most prospects would want more details on the booklet before sending me the money. I could have gotten orders directly from an ad, but I'm sure that I did much better by using the inquiry and follow-up method. I now ask $15.00 for this product.

Prospects need to be sold more if you're asking them to send you $10.00 or more. Mail-order buyers may not hesitate to send you a few dollars (up to $8.00 or so) in direct response to an add, but when the price is $10.00 or more, they usually need more convincing.

In the long run, I advise you to use the inquiry and follow-up method if your product or offer is $8.00 or more. I think the overall results will be better for you. Use your own judgment if your asking price is $5.00 or $6.00. You might try out both methods as a test.

THE SENSE OF NEWNESS AND EXCLUSIVENESS

What about the sense of newness generated by a mail-order product? Buyers everywhere like to know that they're getting something new for their money. They enjoy thinking that a product they order by mail cannot be obtained in regular retail outlets.

Many ads and sales letters for mail-order products and services do, in fact, call attention to the exclusiveness of their product. The ads often make a major point of the fact that the particular item being offered cannot be bought anywhere else. This approach increases the lure of the product. Buyers in general want to order a product all that much more if it is exclusive.

WORD POWER

Whatever your goals or objectives are in the classified ads you write, be aware of the great power of words. The copy you use in your ads can not only increase your immediate income, but it can also help you establish your mail-order business and keep it consistently successful.

Whether you want to get the elements of surprise, newness, curiosity, or value into your ads, words will serve as the major tools of your business. You can pay an ad agency or someone else to write ads for you, but there's a lot to be said for developing a basic skill with words yourself.

If you want to stay in mail order for years to come, one of the smartest things you can do is to fall in love with words. Learn how they can work for you in all kinds of ads. A skill with words in the copy you produce for your products or services could bring you a steady and comfortable income for life—and maybe even make you rich. Strong selling words make for effective ads. And strong ads bring in lots of orders.

Sigmund Freud once summed up the great power of words most effectively: "Words have a magical power. They can bring either the greatest happiness or deepest despair; can transfer knowledge from teacher to student; words enable the orator to sway his audience and dictate its decisions. Words are capable of arousing the strongest emotions and prompting all men's actions."

One way to become more aware of the strongest selling words in ads is to circle the powerful ones you find in magazines and newspapers. Clip these ads out and save them in a special file for future reference.

Now here is another project for you. In the two ads below, circle the strongest words—the ones you believe do the best job of selling. It's alright if you choose several from each section of copy. The first one is from a display ad. The second is a classified ad. Here they are:

HOW TO WIN CONTESTS! Amazing new booklet reveals 15 winning secrets plus suggested forms and letters. Satisfaction guaranteed! $2.00 PPD. (company name and address)

SUCCESS GUIDE THAT MADE ONE MAN WORLD FAMOUS can bring you better money results too! Only $2.00. Order now!! (company name and address)

The words I would have circled in the first ad include "amazing," "new," "winning," "secrets," and "guaranteed." "Satisfaction" is also a good one and could be circled. My best word choices in the second ad are "success," "world famous," "money," and "order now." How many did you circle? Perhaps you circled the same words. Whenever you see ads with strong selling words, cut them out. This will train your mind to be on the alert for them.

CREATING AN AD FROM ONE WORD

As a final example of how a classified ad is created, let's think up another product and do an ad built around just one starting word.

This time, let's say that the item you wish to sell is a game about the world of politics. Let's call this game "Candidate." The asking price is $7.95—guaranteed.

Now here's your assignment. Write a classified ad from either the word "Candidate" or "play." Starting with a verb as the first word in your ad is often better than a noun, but a good classified ad could be started with either word.

Take an hour or so, or an evening if you wish, to try your hand at writing an ad for this game. Don't look at the ad below until you've written one yourself, starting with either word. I'll be taking some time to create an ad myself. Good luck.

The ad I've done appears upside-down in the footnote so you won't be tempted to look at it until you've written your own.*

How did you do with your ad? Count the total number of words in it. Practicing like this is excellent training. Don't expect the first or second ad you write to be perfect. My own ad isn't perfect. Maybe I could do a better one using the word "Candidate" as a starter. You might want to try another ad yourself using "Candidate" first.

The idea behind urging you to write some ads is to get you thinking about the copy, headlines, and selling words for a variety of products. This practice will be very helpful to you when you're ready to write a real ad for your first mail-order product or service.

Refer back to this chapter often when you're planning new ads and creating the copy for them. And keep these points in mind:

1. Ads can be created from a headline or key word.
2. Verbs are often good opening words.
3. Strong copy consists of words and phrases that command attention.
4. Make sure your ad offers a promise. Prospects want to know what your product or offer will do for them. Tell them.
5. Be specific. Stress the key facts of your offer.
6. Ask for action.
7. Try to appeal to human curiosity whenever possible.
8. Practice in the writing of classified ads can be invaluable, and will help you to become established in your business sooner.

Following are five ad "assignments" for you. You can gain some additional experience by writing classified ads for each of them. Take a few days to think about each assignment if you wish. There's no hurry.

---

*Here is the copy I wrote for the game "Candidate." Compare it with your own. I started with the word "play."

Play the Game of Candidate Yourself! Wheel and deal for fun and votes. Only $7.95—guaranteed. Order today!! (my company name, key, and address)

Not bad. The above ad is only 18 words, not counting my company name, key, and address.

Some of these are fictional product items I've dreamed up to give you more practice. A few of them are actually being sold today by mail. Enjoy yourself. You may well be laying the foundation for a prosperous mail-order career. More power to you.

AD ASSIGNMENTS

1. Write a classified ad for a booklet on how to quit smoking priced at $8.00. The booklet is guaranteed.

2. Write a classified ad meant to bring requests for more details about a $9.95 inventor's guide. This is an inquiry and follow-up ad.

3. Write a classified ad for the Sarah Adams Cookbook, priced at $8.95. There's a one-month guarantee on the offer.

4. Write a classified ad for a $5.95 Highway Safety Kit. The kit includes four large posters requesting help in case of accident, sickness, out-of-gas, and mechanical trouble.

5. Assume that you're a record producer. Write an ad offering a service to beginners instructing them on how to make a commercial recording. The asking price is $8.00. No guarantee is included.

10

The Inquiry and Follow-Up Method

The inquiry and follow-up method means just what it says. You run small classified ads stating your offer. Those who are interested in your offer write to you for more details, and then you send them follow-up literature or information concerning your offer. One big advantage of selling this way is that your original ad—run to get prospects to request details from you—usually requires only a few words. You thus save on the cost of advertising.

Here are some examples of the inquiry and follow-up ads currently running in several leading mail-order publications. Notice that most of them offer to send free information:

Exciting, Money-making Opportunity! No experience required! Details 25¢. (address)

CONTROL $1,000,000 IN REAL ESTATE! Net $2,000 monthly! No selling. No capital to start. Unique leverage opportunity. Free brochure. (address)

Start Your Own Correspondence School. Information 50¢. (address)

BUILD YOUR OWN Sofa, Love seat, Chair. Free Brochure. (address)

HOW TO MAKE MONEY in Commercial Art. Information Free! (address)

$50,000 Yearly Possible! Become Financial Broker! Free Details! (address)

Earthworm Profits, Grow in garage, basement! Free literature. (address)

Notice that the first of the ads asks for 25 cents for details on an offer. Some of these ads, designed to get inquiries from prospects, request a small amount of money (usually a few dollars). This money helps a mail-order firm to meet the expense of sending follow-up details to those who request more information. If you receive hundreds of requests for more details, the postage costs can quickly add up. But many interested prospects may not respond to ads that ask for a dollar or more for details on an offer. Most of the inquiry ads you'll see in mail-order magazines and newspapers offer free information—with no charge or strings whatsoever. The reason for this is that many mail-order operators want new prospect names. And these mail-order firms know that by asking for even a small amount of money they may cut down the number of inquiries they'll receive. Your goal in the inquiry and follow-up method is to develop a growing list of customer names. These names can be valuable to you. Why? Simply because you can sell many different offers to these same names. Many customers will buy from you over and over if you treat them right, fill their orders promptly, and offer good products. Many mail-order firms continually run small classified ads offering free details in order to maintain a steady supply of prospect names. So when you use the inquiry and follow-up selling method, it is best to offer details, information, literature, or brochures for free.

INQUIRY AND FOLLOW-UP IS COMPLICATED

By now you've realized that the inquiry and follow-up method of selling is more complicated than selling directly from an ad. Here are some basic reasons why this is so:

1.   Printed sales literature on your product, service, or offer is required. This literature can range from a one-page sales letter to a four-page, two-color booklet.
2.   Order forms are needed, so your customers can easily mail you an order.
3.   A circular that sums up your product or offer is often used in sales literature. Mail-order experts recommend the use of a circular.

4. Specialization is required. This means that strategic copy, illustrations, and a lot of planning are required to describe your offer.

5. Strong sales literature is necessary for high-priced offers such as correspondence courses, which may range in price from $50.00 to $100.00 or more. It's much harder to get a $50.00 order than a $10.00 order.

6. A time lag is involved in receiving orders. Your profits on orders don't come in quickly. You have to send details to those who respond to your ads and then wait for sales.

A GOOD WAY TO LEARN THIS METHOD

I'm a firm believer in learning by doing. I learned a great deal about mail order by testing ads and closely observing the results. I see no reason why you cannot do the same.

If you like the sound of the inquiry and follow-up method and are determined to try it, there's a way you can do it without investing a lot of money. It's the way I first tried this method, and I still use it today for certain products. Here are the steps to follow:

1. Develop a product, service, or offer at a price ranging from $8.95 to $14.95. In this illustration, as in my own case, the product is an informational booklet. I developed a 45-page report and priced it at $10.00.

2. Write the report yourself, as I did, or if you don't want to tackle this alone, you can team up with your spouse or other family member, or even a friend or neighbor. Come up with a good subject for your booklet—something that will have great appeal. There are many possible subjects that will sell for you.

3. Type your booklet neatly, and have some initial copies printed. The more copies you have printed, the more money you will save. Since many offset printers have fairly reasonable prices, you can have 50 or 100 copies printed without spending a lot.

4. Write a *one-page* sales letter (just like you would write to a friend), and type it neatly. Since you're just trying out this inquiry and follow-up method as an experiment, forget about long involved sales literature. As simply as possible, tell what your

Name (please print)	_____
Address	_____
City	_____
State	_____ Zip Code _____
Check	_____ Money Order _____ Cash _____

Figure 10-1

booklet is about and why you believe it will help a prospect. In the last few paragraphs ask for the prospect's order. Near the bottom of the letter leave some space for the prospect's name and address and the manner of payment (see Figure 10-1). Be certain, also, that the full price for your product, service, or offer is quoted somewhere on the order form. If an extra amount is required for postage, say so. If the price is postpaid, then state that on the form. Make it easy for a prospect to send you an order.

5. Have a few hundred copies of your one-page sales letter printed by offset. Black ink on 8½ × 11 size white paper (a good bond paper) is the cheapest. I usually request a 20-pound type paper for most of my printing orders.

6. Run a few test ads in some good mail-order publications *before* you have your booklet printed to see what kind of response you will get on your offer. Use a few words to tell what your booklet is about and offer to send free details in the ad.

7. Send your one-page sales letter (with order form at the bottom) to each prospect who requests more details. Be sure to enclose a business return envelope with each sales letter you mail out.

8. Have your printer on the alert, ready to print your first booklet copies. When you start receiving a number of requests for details, you'll have to decide whether or not to have copies of the booklet printed. A lot of requests for free details means that there's some interest in your offer. Some people will respond out

of curiosity, and after seeing your sales letter, may not send you an order. But others will order if your ads have been run in good mail-order publications and if your sales letter has done its job.

I'm not guaranteeing this is a foolproof system. You may get 25 or 50 requests for details, and you may receive only a few orders from these after you send out your sales letter. On the other hand, you just might do well enough to recoup your expenses and possibly even make a small profit. You will at least be learning this inquiry and follow-up method of selling from actual experience. And if it doesn't work for you the first time, it may work the next time with another offer.

Coordination could be a problem. By this, I mean that before going ahead and having the printing done, you've got to find out if your offer is a dud, if it's lukewarm, or if it's a winner. You'll lose money and be stuck with 50 or more booklets unless you have some idea in advance of how well your offer is going to sell. If requests for details on your offer only trickle in and add up to a disappointing few, you can scrap your plans and save the cost of printing the booklets. You could, of course, have only 10 or 15 booklets printed. Then if your offer doesn't pull well, you're not out as much money. But the cost of printing a few booklets is much higher than printing a lot of booklets. As a rule, the more copies you have printed the more money you save.

You will have to go ahead and have a one-page sales letter printed to send to each request you get for more details. People who buy by mail don't like to wait too long to hear from mail-order companies. The quicker you can get back to them with details on your offer, the better your chances will be for receiving actual orders. If your first sales letter doesn't work, you can chalk up the printing expense as valuable experience you've gained. Maybe your second sales letter will do better.

Orders should be filled promptly. There's a government law in effect requiring mail-order operators to fill orders received (to have them in the mail to customers) within 30 days. The law was passed to protect mail-order buyers who order products and then never receive them or have to wait months before they're filled. Customers who send you an order will expect to receive the item within 30 days or get their money back. The sooner you fill every order and request for details on an offer, the better for your entire business. Try to make it an ironclad rule in your business to fill each order you receive within 24 hours.

Remember this: Some offset printers are very slow in filling their printing orders. They get swamped with orders at times, or a holiday period delays printing. So allow enough time for your material to be printed and shipped to you. You can, of course, save time by phoning your printer to go ahead on a substantial printing order. Some prompt, reliable printers and their current addresses are given in Chapter 1.

IF THERE'S NO RESPONSE TO YOUR SALES LITERATURE

Just because a prospect doesn't respond to your sales literature or letter promptly, it may not mean that you've lost a sale. Send that prospect another sales letter (a duplicate) in two weeks. If there's still no response, keep trying with additional letters every few weeks. On $8.95 to $14.95 priced offers, you should usually hear after the second try, if a prospect is going to buy at all. Higher-priced items may take four or five attempts to get an order.

If the response to your sales literature or letter is poor, you can always either redo it or try an entirely new one. Chapter 12, on sales letters, can help you.

PER INQUIRY SELLING BY RADIO

The advantage of per inquiry selling is that it allows you to see if certain radio stations can produce large numbers of orders for you. If a station is unable to get enough orders, you pay nothing for the air-time used.

This is really a special form of radio advertising used only for certain kinds of products or services. It's still mail order. But instead of your ad appearing in a publication, your offer is advertised on the air, usually in the form of a spot announcement.

In per inquiry selling, you are usually expected to send some information to the station about your product, its benefits, and why you believe it will sell. You offer a discount to the station (about 35 to 40 percent per order received).

Your radio commercial sales message is announced at certain times on the stations. Orders are sent on to you, after the stations deduct their discount rate for advertising your offer.

I have never tried this form of selling, although I did consider it a few times. I don't recommend it to you—at least not at first. I believe that small classified ads are, by far, the best way to launch your business. You can then go on to both display ads and direct mail.

Some mail-order firms claim they have done well using the per inquiry method, but stick to classified ads at first in your business. Later on, after you've grown a little, you might try a per inquiry arrangement with a few stations if you wish. Not every offer is right for radio advertising, however. Lists of stations that will consider working with you in this way can be easily obtained. These stations often advertise in leading mail-order publications.

SUCCESS STORY: Music Career Guide

When I first began to operate my own mail-order business, I discovered through research that some twenty-five million people in the United States alone are trying to write songs and place them with music publishers or record labels. Millions more all over the world are also caught up in the lure of a music career. I knew music well and had years of experience in it, so I spent several months developing the idea of a music career guide.

I used the inquiry and-follow-up method to get prospects. I first ran classified ads in the leading mail-order publications and then sent full information on my music career guide to those who responded. My first few ads brought an avalanche of requests for more details. I quickly sold out of my first printing of the guide. I still sell it for $15.00, and it continues to bring in cash orders through classified ads and also through direct mail. The market for music products is evidently endless.

11

Direct Mail: A Dynamic Selling Tool

A major way of selling your product or service is via direct mail. Direct mail is similar to the inquiry and follow-up method because in both methods you use a sales letter or sales literature to sell your offer. But in direct mail you send your sales material directly to a specific list of qualified names. You don't run an ad to get prospects as in the inquiry and follow-up method.

When selling directly from an ad or by inquiry and follow-up, you receive either orders or inquiries, and from these you obtain your supply of prospect names. But in direct mail, you already have a list of names. You send the information about your offer or your sales literature to each name on the list. Those on the list who wish to buy then mail their orders back to you.

Direct mail is very important to your future in mail order. It could eventually become a virtual goldmine for you. This chapter gives a general idea of what direct mail is about and explains some of the more important aspects in detail.

DIRECT MAIL IN GENERAL

All kinds of companies use direct mail. From large organizations to individuals, many companies use it as a tool to increase the sales of their products or services. Politicians have filled their campaign fund chests for years through the use of direct mail. George Wallace and Ronald Reagan are two examples of politicians who have used direct mail successfully.

Magazine and book publishers use direct mail to increase their sales. For example, Grolier Incorporated launched a $1.3 million advertising campaign to promote *The New Book of Knowledge* (a children's encyclopedia). The company aimed its advertising at over one million families all over the United States. Robert Clarke, the chief executive officer of Grolier, stated the following: "As far as we know, in the mail-order publishing field, this will be the largest launch ever attempted in a new marketing method for a multivolume set."

Hospitals, catalog houses, record companies, stock investment companies, home study and correspondence course firms, insurance companies, missions, and other organizations have all used direct mail successfully. One thing is for sure. These large companies wouldn't continue to send out costly sales literature at considerable postage expense if orders were not being received steadily.

DIRECT MAIL MAKES USE OF MAILING LISTS

The right lists of names—qualified names—are absolutely essential for success in direct mail. You cannot expect to send your sales literature to names on just any list. That would be like using names straight out of a telephone directory. The fact is that not every person is willing to buy by mail. Using "qualified" names means that those receiving your sales literature are known mail-order buyers and are interested in the type of item you're offering. Mailing lists are usually bought or rented from companies known as *list brokers*. The lists generally sell for $50.00 and up per 1,000 names.

Most of the major mailing-list brokers are located in New York City and Chicago. One of the best and quickest ways to check out the quality of mailing lists and obtain current prices is to write to the companies (on your business letterhead) asking for full details. You can easily get the names and addresses of these leading brokers from the Yellow Pages of up-to-date New York and Chicago telephone directories. Most brokers will be happy to send you information about their mailing lists.

The type of mailing list that you will use is a list of known mail-order buyers. When people buy something by mail, their name soon gets included on a mail-order buyers list. A large array of these lists is available. Your success in direct mail will depend largely on your ability to find the most productive mailing lists for your product or offer.

After you've decided which brokers to deal with, your best course of action would be to rent, rather than buy, mail-order lists. If you buy mail-order lists, it will cost you time and money to keep them up to date. Since people often die or move, lists must be updated periodically.

HOW TO SELECT A GOOD MAILING LIST

Here are some helpful pointers in selecting mailing lists:

1. Can you have confidence in the mailing-list broker? Is it a reputable company?
2. Is the rental price fair?
3. Is there an interest or demand for the list?
4. What results have other direct-mail users gotten with the list?
5. What kind of items do the members of the list buy?
6. Is the age of those on the list right for your offer?
7. Is the list up to date with correct addresses?
8. How old is the list? When was the last time the members of the list received an offer for an item similar to yours?

Minimum Orders

Many mailing-list brokers require you to order a minimum number of names. This can be an inconvenience. A minimum order of 5,000 names is typical. At $50.00 and up per 1,000 names, this can be expensive. There are brokers, however, who are glad to rent as few as 1,000 names. The quality of these small lists runs from poor to good, so select your broker carefully. Check out the reputation of prospective brokers and the quality of their lists. You need to get the best prospects that you can for your money.

Testing Mailing-List Names

There are millions of names and all kinds of lists. If you can come up with one offer that sells well, brokers can supply you with an endless number of potential prospects. But rather than send your first mailings to many thousands of names, I suggest that you start small by mailing only to 2,000 or 3,000 names. If the response is encouraging, then you can increase your next mailing to 5,000 or more names. You should go slowly in the early development of your business. If your first test turns out poorly, you'll be glad you didn't go overboard by trying 10,000 names.

Be Suspicious of Mailing Lists

It's wise to be suspicious of mailing lists until you have some substantial proof that their quality is good. With mailing lists selling for cold, hard cash and with so many lists on the market, there's a lot of competition among mailing-list brokers. This competition sometimes results in deceptive sales practices. By not knowing whom you're dealing with or what makes a good list, you can waste a lot of money. If the names on the list you use are phony, "deadwood copies," or are copied from other lists, you're going to lose money, time, postage, and hope. So go slowly. Ask mailing-list brokers you're considering for full information on their lists. And check out the broker's reputation and background in the mail-order business. Again, test with small numbers of names at first. Another good test is to send your sales letters to more than one mailing list. Your sales letters may pull great when sent to one list of names and yet do poorly when mailed to another list. The selection of a high-quality list is essential to your future in direct mail.

Your Best Mailing List

Your most productive and highest-quality mailing list is the growing list of customers who have sent you orders. This list is valuable to you because you can send offers to these customers again and again. If pleased with one of your offers, many customers will buy from you again. So your own list of customers can be your best list of potential buyers.

Mailing-List Sources

Here are some good sources for names of potential direct-mail buyers. Following these are names and addresses of some leading mailing-list brokers.

1. Mailing-list brokers
2. Public records
3. Membership rosters of organizations and associations (Some organizations even sell a directory of their entire membership.)

4. Fraternal, civic, professional, and religious groups
5. Display, classified, and inquiry and follow-up ads
6. Financial rating books
7. Government lists
8. Telephone books (names classified in the Yellow Pages by trade or occupation)

Names Unlimited
183 Madison Avenue
New York, NY 10016

Dunhill List, Incorporated
419 Park Avenue, South
New York, NY 10016

Dependable Lists
333 North Michigan Avenue
Chicago, IL 60601

National Business Lists
295 Madison Avenue
New York, NY 10017

The Kleid Company
200 Park Avenue
New York, NY 10016

MDC List Management
41 Kimler Drive
Hazelwood, MO 63043

THE DIRECT-MAIL PACKAGE

The direct-mail package usually consists of a sales letter, a circular, order form, outer envelope, and reply envelope. Each of these elements of a direct-mail package will be discussed in Chapter 12. Keep in mind that the sales letter is by far the most important part of the total package you send.

SOME EXAMPLES OF DIRECT-MAIL PRODUCTS

Here are some examples of products that have been sold by direct mail. (Some of the products listed can also be sold by the inquiry and follow-up method.)

1. A 17-page sales booklet offering study courses such as "Instant Math," "Double Your Reading Speed in One Week," "Instant Memory Power," "Self-Hypnotism," "Listening Concentration," and "Good Health and Vigor after Fifty" is sent out by

Automated Learning, Incorporated. The price for each course was quoted at $9.98.

2.   A service for inventors is offered by a company in New York. The company sends out a brochure describing the service with an attached reply card. A free "Inventors Information Kit" is sent to those who request it, and all facts and details on the service are offered free of charge.

3.   A secret plan for making money is described in a brochure sent out by another company in New York. A free gift is also offered to anyone ordering. The price is $20.00.

4.   A series of reports on how religion can make a person financially independent is offered for $20.00

5.   A small book on how to be a more effective speaker is offered free to those interested in a course in public speaking. A one-page sales letter brings in requests.

6.   Life, hospital, and accident insurance plans are offered by insurance companies through direct mail. Some of these companies even obtain the birth dates of the people they contact by direct mail. I recently received two sales letters from two different insurance firms. In both cases, the first thing I saw was a policy with my name, birth date, and monthly premium amount clearly stated (they obtain this information from public records). This type of sales letter is clever because it *personalizes* the offer. Both sales letters also stated that the premium can never be raised and that the plans cannot be canceled. There's little doubt that these companies do well with this effective use of direct mail.

SOMETHING TO REMEMBER ABOUT DIRECT MAIL

One great advantage of using direct mail is that it doesn't let all the other mail-order firms know what your offer or product is. Sometimes you may want to see how a special offer will do, and you don't want everyone else in mail order to know about it. Remember: Anyone in this business can see what's offered by simply looking over the mail-order sections of publications. So keep this privacy factor of direct mail in mind. It can be especially useful when you want to test new offers.

DIRECT MAIL CAN BE YOUR ROAD TO RICHES

Sooner or later, direct mail can mean the big time for your mail-order business. Today's newcomer to mail order may well be one of tomorrow's high-stake dealers in direct mail. There are sound reasons why direct mail can be the road to riches for you:

1. You can bring in more responses per 1,000 pieces of mail sent out than by any other medium.
2. You can make your sales package just as simple or sophisticated as you wish. It can range from a one-page sales letter and reply card to a four-page, four-color letter, circular, and order form.
3. You can test your offers or products more often. Different sales letters and combinations of sales literature can bring a variety of responses.
4. You can have a fast-growing list of customers.
5. You can focus on only those prospects who have responded to offers similar to yours. You thus reach qualified prospects. You can also send your mailings only to selected geographic regions.
6. You can send out as many offers as you wish, and you can time your mailings to arrive at any time you want them to.
7. You can send new offers to your growing customer list time after time for extra sales.
8. You can have more freedom in what you say in your direct-mail copy than you can in ads.
9. You can send your offer to individual names, making your sales technique much more personal. Unlike ads, there is no arena effect—ads surrounded by other ads. Your prospects open their mail and there is your sales message—with no other competing ads to lure them away.

On the other hand, you must realize that direct mail is expensive. This is probably its greatest disadvantage. The average cost of getting your mailings in the hands of qualified prospects is currently $200.00 to $400.00 per 1,000. And postage rates are climbing. The cost of sending out direct mail is rising yearly. How expensive your direct mailings are usually depends on how sophisticated and elaborate your total package turns out to be. You can save money by sending out simple mailings, but doing so may cut down the number of orders you receive.

THE HUGE PROFIT POTENTIAL OF DIRECT MAIL

Direct mail has an enormous profit potential because it's entirely possible to obtain lists of millions of prospective names. Even if the response to any one mailing is small, you always have millions of other names to try with your offer. There's no end to sources of names. But a word of warning is in order here. Don't jump into direct mail and attempt to reach a large number of names unless your product or offer has widespread interest. To reach millions, your offering must have strong mass appeal. Since the postage bill for sending out a mailing to millions of names would be huge, a good way to start out is to test your offer with a few thousand qualified names. If the return response is good and orders come in steadily, you can then increase your mailing to many thousands of names. But find your break-even point first.

I have stated that millions of names can possibly bring you a bonanza because I want you to realize that the potential for huge direct-mail profits always exists. But, of course, you first have to find out if you have a good pulling offer and direct-mail package. Once you know you've got a winner, it's exciting to think about all the other millions of names you can send your mailing to for possible sales. When based on a mailing sent to millions of names, even a small percentage response can turn into a whopping number of orders. When the product or offer is right and backed by a large mailing, the profits in direct mail can be staggering.

SELLING BY CATALOG

Most mail-order operators dream of having their own catalog someday. They would like to repeat the success story of Sears, Roebuck and Company. But catalog selling is not for beginners. It takes a lot of experience in mail order, careful planning, and above all the right merchandise. I advise you to try selling by catalog only after you've made some progress in your business, sold by classified ads or direct mail, and developed an overall understanding of the industry. In time, and through the experience of running your own company, you will get a feeling for what prospects will buy by catalog. But I do urge you to learn now all you can about catalog selling. Write to companies that advertise free catalogs and look over these catalogs carefully. This will give you a good idea of the variety of catalogs now being offered.

Preprinted Catalogs

Many newcomers to mail order are tempted to send out preprinted catalogs. In this setup you buy ready-made catalogs that have your own company name and address printed on them. The company that sells you the catalogs handles all the paperwork for you and ships the products ordered. The catch in this type of operation is that thousands of others are mailing similar catalogs selling the same items. If profits were as good as some of these companies claim, the companies wouldn't need mail-order dealers to send out their catalogs; they would send the catalogs out themselves. Some of these companies that sell preprinted catalogs are also in the mailing-list business. These preprint companies sell mailing lists to the same people who buy their catalogs. So it's obvious who makes the best profits—the companies selling the preprinted catalogs and the mailing lists.

So don't fall for dealer operations like this. You can do far better selling your own mail-order products and offers. And in time, you might develop a catalog of your own.

Response to Catalogs

When considering selling by catalog, you'll increase your chances for a good response by waiting until you've developed a considerable list of customers. Catalogs sent to a cold list of names never do as well as catalogs mailed to your own proven list of customers. Of course, you can sell catalog merchandise with the right broker by using a good quality mailing list. But it takes time to build a list from your classified ads. So sell by catalog only after you have accumulated a large list of customers.

Studying Catalogs

As you build your own list you can be planning and thinking about your first catalog. Send for catalogs and collect them in a special file marked "Catalogs for Future Reference." Look over the catalogs carefully and refer to them often. Ask yourself the following questions about each one:

1. How many items are offered in the catalog?

L.L.Bean ®

Outdoor Sporting Specialties

L.L.Bean®

Christmas 1984

FREE
Christmas
Catalog

Features active and casual wear for men and women who enjoy the outdoors. Winter sports equipment, luggage and furnishings for home or camp. Practical and functional gift ideas. All fully guaranteed to give 100% satisfaction. Our 72nd year of providing dependable mail order service.

☐ **Send FREE Christmas Catalog**

Name_____

Address_____

City_____

State_____Zip_____

L. L. Bean, Inc.
8471 Spruce St., Freeport, ME 04033

L. L. Bean is one of the most successful mail-order companies in the nation.

2.   What is the average price of a catalog item?
3.   Are the catalog items guaranteed?
4.   Are the catalog items appealing to most people?

5.   Are the catalog items available in stores?
6.   Are there any items that would stimulate repeat sales and influence customers to buy similar products?
7.   Is the catalog printed in black and white or in color?
8.   Is the catalog durable enough to hold up to a lot of handling?

Catalog Buying Is Growing

A good reason to begin thinking about a catalog of your own is that ordering by catalog is becoming increasingly popular. The *New York Times* recently reported that "the century old practice of catalog shopping is booming. Consumers representing all income levels and interests (from insurance to correspondence courses) are attracted by mail-order catalogs." Proof of this catalog buying boom is reflected in the Montgomery Ward catalog, which is sent yearly to over six million consumer households.

Your Minicatalog

There's an easy way to get into catalog selling if you insist on trying it. You don't need a 35-page, three-color catalog to bring in orders. All you need is a one-page minicatalog. My first catalog was one sheet of paper listing seven items. The argument can be made that a one-page list of items is not a real catalog. In the traditional view of what catalogs are supposed to be, this is true. But from my own point of view, it is a catalog. The point is, there's nothing to keep you from listing all of your offers on a one-page sheet.

Once you decide to use a one-page catalog, have it printed and include it in your regular mail-order package. This is the same way that regular full-size catalogs are sent to prospects. Whenever you communicate with a prospect, send along your one-page minicatalog. You should receive many additional orders.

Your Second Catalog

You can eventually build a much better catalog from this minicatalog. But using this one will get you thinking about catalogs in general. It will give you experience in describing your products or services. It will prove to you that enclosing catalogs brings in extra orders, and encourage you to develop a better one in the future. Many catalogs develop this way from very small beginnings.

Your second catalog may need two pages or more to describe all of your items. From this point on there's no limit to the amount of merchandise you can sell by mail. You should be sure, however, that there's a market for each item you add to your catalog. A continuous study of what's being offered in other catalogs can be a valuable guide in selecting your own items. Most successful catalogs have one strong characteristic—variety. Although you can't possibly have something for everyone and will probably never compete with Sears and Roebuck, try to have some variety in your catalog.

A catalog of your own that continues to expand and grow yearly is one way to a fortune in direct mail. It often takes years of experience, but fortunes are being made today from catalog sales. Again, until you have experience in operating your mail-order business, I strongly urge you to delay any plans for a catalog. You first need the thrill and encouragement of selling profitably by classified ads. But keep it in mind. It can be your ace in the hole for the future. And who knows? It may just be the card that wins you a fortune in orders.

DIRECT-MAIL SALES LITERATURE

The key parts of a direct-mail package are a sales letter, order form, circular, and reply envelope. Leaving out any one of these may reduce the number of orders you receive.

Next, we'll take a look at each of these essential parts of a direct-mail package. When you decide to try a direct mailing, you'll want to have a basic understanding of all of them.

12

The Direct-Mail Package

THE SALES LETTER

The most important part of any direct-mail package is the sales letter. Don't ever forget it. The order form, circular, brochure, and reply envelope add extra pulling strength, but the sales letter is the persuasive tool that leads a prospect to send you an order. A good sales letter is like money in the bank.

Millions of people everywhere receive direct mail each week or even daily. A lot of it gets thrown away, but you'd be surprised at how many people actually read sales letters.

If a sales letter can grab attention with an appealing headline or opening, a prospect will probably read the first paragraph of the letter. If interest is still held, most of the letter will probably be read. Getting attention is absolutely vital, and is the first goal of a sales letter.

A sales letter is somewhat like a Seeing Eye dog. Prospects are "blind" when they first open a piece of direct mail; they don't have the foggiest idea what is being offered. But they do know that someone is trying to sell them something. So their sales resistance is called into play.

A friend of mine recently received eight pieces of "junk mail" (as he called them) on a single day. These offers tried to get him to buy land in Florida, subscribe to two magazines, increase his hospital insurance, and receive a stock investment newsletter.

The point is this. To compete with all the other direct mail a prospect receives in a week's time, your sales letter has to be strong. A professional, well-planned sales letter can put your offer head and shoulders above the others. Your offer will stand out like a lighthouse in the darkness.

How to Make a Good Sales Letter

Here's how to make a strong sales letter:

1. Design an effective letterhead. Few prospects will react to a letter printed on plain paper without a company name and address at the top. Black and white letterheads can pull orders, but one or two colors usually bring better results.
2. Make your letter friendly. Cold, lifeless letters go nowhere.
3. Use letter-size (8½ × 11), 20-pound paper stock. Again, colored paper is better. In my own business, I found that women respond to the color pink, and men to the color blue, but there's no hard-and-fast rule to this. You can test different colors of paper and ink to see what works best. Some operators report good results using plain white paper with black ink.
4. Avoid wordiness and long, involved paragraphs. The best sales letters look inviting to read. Underline words for emphasis and indent paragraphs. Keep the total effect of your letter simple. Orders come from easy-to-read letters.
5. Have your printing done on one side of the paper only for best results. But for a four-page letter, you can hold the paper cost down by printing on both sides of a sheet. Some letters still seem to pull well even when printed on both sides and without any colors. It's what your letter says that counts the most. But do try to keep your letter neat and professional-looking.
6. Many sales letters still open with "dear friend"; some others open with "dear customer." You can do the same or skip the greeting entirely.
7. Be as specific as possible when explaining your offer.
8. Try to appeal to a prospect's emotions and dominant desires.
9. Use a P.S. at the end of your sales letter. Make this P.S. a strong appeal for action, or a reminder of any bonus gift you are offering. Never underestimate the power of a strong P.S.

You Can Learn to Write Good Sales Letters

One sure way to a fortune in direct mail is to develop a skill for writing sales letters that will pull orders. Once you know how to do this, you can write your own ticket. There are many corporations that will be happy to send you large checks for writing their sales letters. So this ability is well worth developing.

Sales letters are big business. Since they are an excellent way to deliver a sales message, many large companies use them consistently to increase their overall profits. You could offer your services to one of these companies. Or you could use this valuable skill for yourself by writing sales letters for your own offers. Some people make money both ways. But keep this in mind: Most companies that will give you an assignment to write a sales letter will only pay you a flat fee for your service. This means that even though you get $700.00 or $1000.00 to write a sales letter for a company, that firm might turn around and make a fortune by using your letter.

So when you perfect the skill of creating sales letters, you'll be smarter to use your talent to make money for yourself. One strong sales letter can pull enough orders to raise your bank account considerably. Some letters can bring you so many orders that you'll have to hire outside help to get all your mail opened. I'm talking about strong sales letters that motivate prospects to send you orders at once. So set a goal now to develop a sharp ability to plan and write sales letters. Once you have a letter that brings in stacks of orders, you may choose to forget about classified ads and stick with direct mail from then on.

Ad Copy versus Sales Letters

You may discover that you do far better writing sales letters than you do writing copy for ads. Some individuals freeze when they try to sit down and write ad copy. Maybe the word "copy" scares them. Basic sales technique applies to copy for both ads and sales letters, but some people seem to be much better at planning and writing a sales letter. It's easier to be informal in a friendly sales letter. And you certainly have more space in a letter to tell your story. You should try writing both kinds of copy. After you've tried both ad copy and sales letters, you may decide to use one exclusively or both simultaneously.

A Proven Plan for Learning to Write Good Sales Letters

I would like to suggest a plan for learning to write good sales letters that has worked well for me. This plan was developed from a study of the principles of direct-mail selling, the knowledge and methods of suc-

WILBUR ENTERPRISES
1763 Autumn Avenue
Memphis, Tennessee 38112

THE BEST JOB IN THE WORLD COULD BE YOURS - CREATING ALL KINDS OF MONEY-MAKING IDEAS!

Dear Friend:

I'm sure you'll agree that the best job in the world would be one in which you work for yourself, set your own hours, live anywhere you wish, and see your income rise or double year after year. IT COULD ALL BE YOURS!

What could be more wonderful than being paid well to create all kinds of ideas? You're the boss...in business for yourself.

I'm talking about your own creative idea business. I've had my own for over 10-years and see no reason why you can't do the same by following my simple plan.

Millions of people everywhere have to drag themselves to work each day. They dislike their work and feel trapped in a dead-end job. It's a sheer waste of time and human energy.

My simple directions on how to start and run your own creative business can put checks in your mail-box day after day. And finding money in your mail is always a delight!

My plan is no mail-order scheme. There are no ads to buy or run, no name lists to get, no circulars to print or stock merchandise to keep. I fell for such worthless mail-order offers myself years ago and wasted money on them. So I'm not about to cheat anyone this way...or any other.

My plan is a proven way to tap the creative ability now within you and make it pay off for you in many ways. I show you exactly HOW TO increase your creative powers and make them work for you in the form of MONEY-MAKING ideas.

I've been well paid for many years to create new ideas. You can do the same thing.

I'm no tycoon...just an ordinary person who got tired of slaving for other companies, inconsiderate bosses, and working in jobs with little or no future.

I dreamed of having my own business for years. One day I said goodbye to the 9 to 5 life and struck out on my own. I've never been sorry. In fact, I've been much happier ever since. I have complete creative freedom in my

-2-

own business. And my business and income continue to grow each year.

I WANT THE SAME THING TO HAPPEN TO YOU. Your success in your own creative idea business will be no competition to mine..simply because there are too many markets all paying well for new ideas. Why should I be greedy?

What ideas do you create? All kinds. Greeting cards (at $25 to $50 per accepted idea), short filler articles easy to do, newspaper and magazine articles-features, art and advertising ideas, new toy ideas, short stories, books, textbook ideas, fashion ideas, songs, poems, TV scripts, new inventions, sales ideas (if you sell anything for a living), and many more.

All the above ideas and more are in demand and pay from $25 or $50 up to THOUSANDS OF DOLLARS and/or royalty contracts.

You send these ideas to the editors and executives of such companies, publications, newspapers, and firms. They're waiting with OPEN CHECK-BOOKS to send you good money for ideas they can use.

The only way you use the mail is sending your ideas to the right places. IT COSTS YOU NOTHING but the time and paper to create these new ideas..plus the postage to send them on their way. You can start part-time now if you wish (for an EXTRA INCOME) and go full-time later.

But first you have to become more creative and alert to new ideas. My proven plan will make you more creative within days. I also name some key places (markets) where you can start sending ideas.

Is it really possible to build a good income with creative ideas? I'm the proof that it is. I've created thousands of such ideas and sent them out all over the world. I've had lots of fun doing it and been well paid.

There's ONE RISK. Once creating new ideas for MONEY gets in your blood, it may ruin you for doing any other type of work. THERE'S JUST NOTHING LIKE BEING YOUR OWN BOSS IN A PROFITABLE BUSINESS THAT'S ALSO FUN!

One more thing. When you send me the enclosed PINK ORDER FORM and a money order, I will send your copy of my plan BY RETURN MAIL. Personal checks take about two weeks to clear. We fill all orders (sent with money order) THE SAME DAY THEY'RE RECEIVED.

Your satisfaction with my plan is guaranteed or I will refund your money.

Yours sincerely,

L. Perry Wilbur

P.S. My idea business now brings me a monthly annuity...a certain amount of money to start each month. It could do the same for you!

cessful mail-order operators, and the experiences I have had in writing and using sales letters. The key word in any plan of this type is "practice." Planning and writing sales letters is like playing the guitar—there's always a lot more to learn. You will discover this for yourself as you learn to write good sales letters.

First, read and study various sales letters that are being used today. A quick way to get these sales letters is to answer a number of ads that offer free details and the letters will be delivered to your mailbox. Before long, your name will be on several direct-mail lists, and you will be bombarded with sales letters and literature for all kinds of products and offers. You're probably already receiving a number of direct-mail offers. Don't throw them away; save the sales letters for future reference. In a short time, you'll have a thick folder of letters to study.

Second, from the letters you've collected, choose one you think is particularly strong. Copy it down word for word to get a feel for the psychology, rhythm, style, and content. It's better to write in longhand rather than typing it. This way you'll acquire a better understanding of the overall thought process behind it.

You may be thinking that this sounds like a lot of tedious work. It does take some time and effort to copy a sales letter in full, but I can personally vouch for this method of learning. It will, in time, ingrain in your mind the method for planning and writing sales letters. Believe me, there's no better or faster way to develop this ability.

When I first used this plan I sometimes got tired of copying letters, but I began to realize that this effort was teaching me a lot about sales letters and why they make prospects buy. I know that you can do the same.

Third, after you feel that you really know the first letter well, pick a second letter and copy it. After doing this, copy as many letters as you can, but set a limit of 20 copies for each letter. If you really don't feel that you know a letter by then, continue to make more copies. Don't worry about the time it takes; there's no hurry. You're copying each letter to learn.

Continue to copy sales letters for at least a year. This is, of course, while you follow your regular routine. Fit the copying into your daily or weekly schedule. If you can keep copying for a year, you will have learned a great deal about what goes into a sales letter.

If all this seems like a big price to pay for developing the skill of writing sales letters, keep in mind that one sales letter, which you plan and create yourself, could bring you a fortune. You can use this ability time and again in your mail-order business. If one letter doesn't pull big for you, another one may hit.

You won't, of course, know all there is to learn about sales letters after a year of copying them. You could spend five or 10 years studying these sales messages and still not scratch the surface. But you'll certainly know enough to write an effective letter when selling one of your own products or services by direct mail. And sometimes one successful item is all you need to bring in a cash-order jackpot.

Fourth, try writing a new sales letter of your own every few weeks or so while you are doing your copying. You might first try to do a short, one-page letter. After you write it, go over it. Compare your letter with some of the letters you've been copying. Where does your letter look good or weak? Ask yourself how you could improve it. Be willing to rewrite it. Take as long as you wish, but get it into the strongest shape possible. When you feel certain that you cannot improve on your own sales letter any more, type it. Then think about having your sales letter printed and trying it out on direct mail prospects.

It's unlikely that the first sales letter you write will be strong enough to do well for you. You will probably need additional practice. I promise you this: If you keep your copying practice going and continue to write your own sales letters, you're going to reach the point in six months to a year where you can create a sales letter that will pull orders by direct mail.

Finally, apply your skill in writing sales letters to your own products, services, or offers. When you come up with a letter that you know is an effective seller, use it.

I'm sure you can successfully use this plan. By copying existing sales letters, and at the same time planning, experimenting with, and writing new sales letters of your own, you can obtain an independent income via direct mail. And if one of your sales letters hits big, you could find yourself in the mail-order big leagues.

Sales Letters That Pull

What do sales letters and people who sell face-to-face have in common? The answer is the sales process itself. In most cases, an effective sales letter will follow the same path to a sale that the person-to-person sales professional uses. This sales process consists of four important steps: attention, interest, conviction, and action. To complete a sale, all four steps must be employed. Learn to master each of them, and your future in selling direct mail is assured.

Attention. The first step in the sales process is attention. Just like a classified or display ad, a direct-mail sales letter must command the reader's attention. So let's look at some examples of headlines, greetings, and opening lines taken from several sales letters currently being mailed:

- I'll Give You the Power to Get Rich Free! (money plan)
- Dear Dweller in the Universe (greeting from a test program for psychic powers)
- Montgomery Ward is pleased to announce a direct marketing opportunity that has never been offered before. (catalog advertising sales offer)
- Learn to Meditate Correctly, Easily and Naturally with an Expert in the Teaching Field! (headline promoting a meditation workshop)
- So many great things have been happening with our winners that we can confidently say that American Song Festival competitions are truly an "open door" to the music industry. (international songwriting competition)
- How would you like to be rich—starting almost immediately— without effort, without experience, without risk? (opening line from wealth-building system)
- Have you ever agonizingly pushed your legs from the warmth of a cozy bed on a cool morning and groaned to yourself, "Oh no, not another day"? (magazine subscription)

Interest. The second step in the sales process is to arouse interest. Many letters accomplish this within a few paragraphs; other letters take a full page to do it. Do your best to get the prospect interested in your product or offer. And do it in just a few paragraphs.

How do you stimulate interest? By letting the readers of your sales letters know that what you have to offer is important, timely, helpful, profitable, or useful to them. Prospects want to know the benefits of your offer. They will read the first paragraph and then decide whether to read more or tear it up. So your goal is to whet the interest of your prospects so they'll want to read more.

Self-identification is a powerful tool in arousing interest, and you should use it. If prospects can identify with the content of the first few paragraphs, they will be motivated to read on. I call this type of arousal the "you appeal." Through the "you appeal," you can prove to your prospects that it's worth their time to read more of your letter.

Here are several examples of opening paragraphs from effective sales letters. Notice how each one uses the "you appeal" and sums up the promise, benefit, and overall value of the product or offer.

- From a sales letter offering a way to make money:

I'm sure you'll agree that the best job in the world would be one in which you work for yourself, set your own hours, live anywhere you wish, and see your income rise or double year after year. IT COULD ALL BE YOURS!

- From a sales letter offering a report on how to get more out of life through walking:

Once Your Legs Go, Can the Rest Be Far Behind?

Got the tummy ache, backache, headache, the blues, that tired run-down feeling? Whatever it is that may be ailing you, walking will make you feel better.

- From a sales letter offering a system for creating new ideas:

If you would like to increase your income each and every year—and have a wonderful time doing it by creating your own original ideas—then let me explain how I learned to do it.

Whenever you sit down to plan and write a new sales letter, keep the following advice in a place where you can see it at all times: Your sales letter is received by an *individual*. You may send out thousands of letters, but each one will be read by an individual.

Popular radio and television personality Arthur Godfrey built a brilliant broadcasting career through his ability to make each member of a large audience feel and believe that commercial messages were directed only to themselves. He spoke and communicated to each listener as an individual. This me-to-you feeling was a major reason for his huge success.

Conviction.   The third step in the sales process is conviction. You must convince a prospect that what you're offering has real value and is worth the price you're asking. Your goal here is to make prospects see themselves using and benefiting from your offer now—not some time in the future. Creating an image in the mind of a prospect is a way to instill this conviction. Try to use words and sentences that will create pictures in a prospect's mind. A good example of this is recreational vehicle sales. Salespeople sell these vehicles to prospects on a face-to-face basis. But think how the use of this type of item can create pictures in a prospect's mind. Remember: The human mind thinks in pictures. Superior selling, whether by mail or face-to-face, creates clear and attractive pictures in a prospect's mind. When prospects see themselves on the road traveling in style in a trailer and having the time of their lives, they will be strongly motivated to buy. So help prospects see themselves using your product or offer and benefiting from it in some way.

Another way to establish conviction is to get a prospect to agree to a series of points being made in your sales letter. It's psychologically hard for a prospect to think yes to a series of questions and then suddenly arrive at a no. Use points or questions that bring a yes response. Here is one example: "Wouldn't you like to bank more money each month, own your own part-time business, and be on the road to financial independence?" Try to phrase your questions in a fresh way, however, as many have been overused.

Many sales letters have a positive flavor. They are written in a way that assumes a prospect can see the value of an offer and will buy it. This kind of positive impression in a sales letter is hard for many prospects to resist. A natural tendency in life is to think negatively. An upbeat sales letter just might be the most positive thing some people see all day. So try to saturate your letters with positivism and enthusiasm. The two go hand in hand and can work together to establish conviction. Once prospects feel convinced about your offer, they are ready for the last step of the sales process—the appeal for action.

Action.   The final step in the sales process is action. Every good ad has an appeal for action, and the same is true for a direct-mail sales letter. Getting attention, arousing interest, and establishing conviction are mostly wasted without it. You want prospects to send you an order as soon as they finish reading your letter. So an appeal for action is a must.

Here are some examples of appeals taken from direct-mail sales letters. Some of the following have proved to be highly successful:

Please use the enclosed envelope now. (subscription offer)

Now the choice is yours, throw this letter away and forget it as I once did, or prepare to embark on one of the most exciting adventures of your life. (a system for building wealth)

We sincerely hope that you will read over the enclosed entry forms. IT COULD BE THE BREAK YOU'VE BEEN LOOKING FOR! (The American Song Festival Competition)

The Circle of the Mystic and Occult Arts can open the door to this new life for you. I invite you to sign the Reservation Card and return it today. (membership organization)

If you are interested, please let us know right away as our supply is pretty slim. Just verify that we have your correct name and address, and send the correct amount in cash or check for the number of reports you want. We'll send them promptly by return mail. (report on family names)

If you are interested, please let me know right away as I have only ordered a small press run. You can order by using the coupon at the bottom of this page. (report on government benefits)

Send for the book today. Remember, now more than ever you have a real money fight on your hands and it is only going to get worse. Here is a chance to put the odds on your side. (book)

Be sure to add a P.S. at the end of your sales letter. Think of it as having a last word with someone who is reading your letter. A P.S. can greatly increase the chances that potential customers will send you an order. Some direct-mail experts claim that a sales letter with an appealing P.S. at the end will outpull a letter without one by two to one. A P.S. is frequently used to offer a free item or bonus to those prospects who send in orders. Here are some examples of the use of the P.S. taken from existing sales letters:

P.S.   For a FREE copy of the ASF's 112-page *Song-writing Notebook*, just write to me and I'll make sure it is mailed to you immediately. (American Song Festival Competition)

P.S.   They say the "Proof is in the pudding." Remember, that is exactly what I can do. One final word: this most unusual club is kept small with select members all over the world. You will not be given another chance to become a member. (wealth accumulation plan)

Bonus Extra—To get you off to a good winning start, I am including with each order a detailed analysis of two of the best trading opportunities in commodities at the present time. (commodity trading system)

Here is a P.S. taken from one of my own sales letters. This particular letter has been a strong order puller every time I've used it. And the P.S. adds extra power to the total effect of the letter:

> P.S.   We send this guidebook to you with our GUARANTEE. You may return it within 14 days after receiving it for a full money-back refund. Get the order form below into the mail now for your valuable copy of There's a Place for You in Music. You'll be glad you did.

I went all out in this sales letter. After the above P.S., I also added the following:

> Bonus Gift—Send your order within the next 10 days and we'll include a FREE BONUS GIFT that will help you the rest of your life—whatever your career goals or life goals may be.

A Sales Letter Example

You now know the four key elements of an effective sales letter and have seen some good examples. Now let's construct an actual sales letter. First we need a product or service. So let's say, for example, that the product is an instructional booklet on making money by writing and selling original articles. This product should be called a *report* rather than a booklet. A report sounds more impressive. I have enthusiasm for this type of product and have considered selling it myself. I want to emphasize that whatever you sell by mail, pick something that interests you greatly. Your sales letter will reflect this enthusiasm. Remember: The techniques of effective sales letter writing used in this example apply to any mail-order item.

There are millions of amateur writers everywhere interested in writing for pay, so a report on this topic might do well. The sales letter in this example is two pages long. Before you start writing a sales letter, you should decide on its length. But any length can be tried by writing separate letters for the same offer. You learn a lot by experimenting.

Any time you need help in writing your letters, refer back to this example. It is organized into sections with all the key parts listed.

Who knows? This report on writing articles for money might turn out to be a direct-mail winner.

1. Headline: We need an attractive headline to grab attention as soon as a reader opens the sales letter. Here is one that might work:

Writing Original Articles Is a Surefire Way to Boost Your Income and Be Your Own Boss—Either Part-time or Full-time!

2.   Greeting: This part of the letter is optional. Many sales letters don't use a greeting at all. It's up to you. I have used one in most of my own letters.
     Here's the greeting for this example:

Dear Friend:

3.   Attention-getting opening: Remember: The first few paragraphs determine whether a prospect reads your letter or not. Get the reader's attention fast. Here is the opening I'll use:

If you would like to write and sell your own articles for *cash,* then let me explain how I learned to do it and why I am so sure you can do it for profit too.

What do you think of this opening? Read it over again. It's short, to the point, and tells the reader at once what the offer is all about.

4.   Section to arouse interest:

I started writing 12 years ago. I thought of it at first as just a part-time hobby. But I soon fell in love with the writer's way of life.

Six years ago, I made the decision to write full-time. I haven't been sorry. In fact, every day has been a new adventure.

I haven't struck it rich yet as a writer. But I've made a very good living. And I've done it my way.

If you like your work, the money usually takes care of itself. It's your life that counts the most—how you spend your days.

I do all kinds of articles—from general interest material to profiles of famous people.

The first year I went full-time I missed that regular paycheck. But I sold 50 articles. I was proud. And I knew I would do better.

Last year I wrote and sold 200 articles. That's a lot of sales. But I know I can do even better. The future looks great.

You can make money as an article writer—just as I do—and have fun too. You can write when and where you want to and as much as you choose.

Article writing for profit can fit into the life you're now living.

You can write three articles a year or several hundred. You can write early in the morning or late at night. You're the boss.

Become an article writer and you will seldom be bored. You will get out in the world and talk to all kinds of people.

5. Section to establish conviction:

There are *eight* basic types of articles you can write. So you always have a variety of kinds of articles you can do.

It's a great life. Everything you do and everywhere you go can be possible subjects for articles. When you're an article writer, you wake up in the morning enthused. Life is exciting. The whole world looks fascinating to an article writer.

My first published article 12 years ago brought me only $7.00. But seeing my article and name in print that first time was a big thrill. Something clicked inside me that day. I knew I would be an article writer for life.

I can help you write and sell your own articles for *cash*. In the 12 years I've been an article writer, I've sold thousands of articles and features to magazines and newspapers. I must be doing something right.

I've even had articles published in far off places like Hong Kong, England, Australia, New Zealand, Mexico, and South Africa.

When you become a selling article writer, THE ENTIRE WORLD is your market.

After 12 years of opening letters with checks in them for my articles, I still come running when I hear the mail carrier arriving. Mail call is the HIGHLIGHT of my day.

AND I WANT THE SAME THING TO HAPPEN TO YOU. It can—and sooner than you think.

I've developed a system for writing and selling all kinds of articles. This report is based on my proven success as a professional. To get my system to you at the lowest possible cost, I've had it printed in easy-to-read report form on plain, white paper.

6.   Section for appeal for buying action:

If you really want to write and sell your own articles for money part-time now—and maybe full-time later—then mail the order form to me today. I'll send you my report on writing articles for cash by return mail.

Then *you* decide if you want to order the additional materials I offer on how to specialize in certain article fields.

I *guarantee* your satisfaction with my article-writing system or I will refund your money at once.

7.   Closing: I'll use the close I like best and one that has worked well for me—"Best regards." You're free, of course, to use "sincerely," "very truly yours," or whatever you wish.

8.   P.S.: Here is a good one for this report:

P.S.   Today's mail alone brought me three checks for magazine arti-cles, one newspaper feature acceptance, and four replies from editors expressing interest in new article ideas. Send the order form now and start *your own* writing success.

There you have it. A two-page letter has been created. There's no way of knowing how well this letter would sell without printing it and sending it out as part of a direct-mail package to qualified prospects. But this is a good example of an actual sales letter written to sell a specific product via direct mail. Use it as a guide when doing your own sales letters.

Notice that there are no long or wordy sections in this letter. Wordy letters are hard to read. Keep paragraphs short. The same goes for sen-tences—use simple ones. Avoid long or technical words. The easier and more appealing your sales letter is to read, the better the chances are that prospects will read all the way through it, become interested in your offer, and take action on the spot by sending you an order.

When you've written a sales letter that pulls, you'll certainly know it. The orders will flow in steadily or even in a flood. And that's when you'll know that all the planning and writing have been worth it. You'll have a pulling sales letter, and that's the best kind.

WILBUR ENTERPRISES
1765 Autumn Avenue
Memphis, Tennessee 38115

Dear Friend:

If you would like to write and sell your own articles for cash money, then let me explain how I learned to do it.

And why I am so sure you can do it too.

I started writing 12-years ago. I thought of it at first as just a part-time hobby. But I soon fell in love with the writer's way of life.

Three years ago, I made the decision to write full-time. I haven't been sorry. In fact, every day has been a new adventure.

I haven't struck it rich yet as a writer. But I've made a very good living. And I've done it my way.

Like the work that you're doing, and the money usually takes care of itself. It's your life that counts the most...how you spend your days. I write articles full-time. I do all kinds...from general interest articles to profiles of famous people.

The first year I went full-time I missed that regular pay-check. But I sold 50-articles. I was proud. And I knew I would do better.

Last year I wrote and sold 145-articles. That's a lot of sales. But I know I can do even better. The future looks great!

You can make money as an article writer...just as I do..and have fun too. You can write when and where you want to and as hard as you choose.

Article writing can fit into whatever life you're now living.

You can write three articles a year, twenty, or several hundred.

You can write in the early morning or late at night. You're the boss! You will get out in the world and talk to all kinds of people.

Become an article writer and you will seldom be bored. You will get out in the world and talk to all kinds of people.

There are eight basic types of articles you can write. So you always have a variety of kinds of articles you can do.

It's a great life. Everything you do and everywhere you go can be possible subjects for articles from your pen. When you're an article writer, you wake up in the morning enthused. Life is exciting.

The whole world looks fascinating to an article writer.

My first published article 12-years ago brought me only $7.00. But seeing my article and name in print that first time was a big thrill.

Something clicked inside me that day. I knew I was an article writer

---

for life.

I can help you write and sell your own articles for cash money. In the 12-years I've been an article writer, I've sold thousands of articles-features to magazines and newspapers. I must be doing something right.

I've even had articles published in far off places like Hong Kong, England, Australia, New Zealand, Mexico, and South Africa.

When you become a selling article writer, the entire world is your market.

After 12-years of opening letters with checks in them for my articles, I still come running when I hear the postman arriving. Mail-call is the highlight of my day.

And I want the same thing to happen to you. It can..sooner than you think.

I've developed a system for writing and selling all kinds of articles. This 6-part system is based on my proven success as a full-time professional.

To get my system to you at the lowest possible cost, I've had each part printed in easy-to-read form on plain white paper. If you like part one, you can order and go on to part 2 - 6.

You order each part of the system separately...one at a time..when you decide you want it. You move at your own speed this way.

If you really want to write and sell your own articles for money... part-time now and maybe full-time some day..then mail the order form to me today. I'll send you part one of my system by return mail.

Then you decide if you want to order part two. What could be fairer?

I guarantee your satisfaction with this system or I will refund your money at once.

Kindest regards,

L. Perry Wilbur

P.S. Today's mail alone brought me 3-checks for magazine articles, a newspaper feature acceptance, and 4-go-aheads from editors on new article ideas. Send the pink order form now for Part I and start your own writing success.

3 FREE EXTRAS! A free guide-sheet is sent with part one.
    . when you order part 3, free marketing for one of your
      articles is offered.
    . A free market report is offered when you order part 6.
  • For still more proof, read over the enclosed blue insert.

A Two-page Sales Letter

161

THE ORDER FORM

The main thing to keep in mind about the order form in a direct-mail package is convenience. A carefully designed order form will make it easier for prospects to order while saving you money. One of my sales letters has the order form printed on the bottom of one side so that prospects can detach the form and send it in the return envelope with their payment.

If you decide to build the order form into your sales letter, be sure to leave enough space for the customer's name, address, city, state, country, and zip code. Have lines printed after and between these entries to indicate where information is to be filled in. If the order form is printed on the same side of the paper as the sales message, have a dotted line printed on that side between the message copy and the form. This lets the customer know that this is the order form to be completed and separates it from the sales copy.

You might wish to have a pair of scissors sketched in and shown clipping the order form along the dotted line. This can often influence the prospect to go ahead and send you an order. Also request on the order form that the customer's name and address be printed. A printed name and address will save you the trouble of trying to figure out correct

---

```
              FREE  TRIAL  CERTIFICATE
WILBUR ENTERPRISES
1763 Autumn Avenue, Memphis, Tennessee 38112

My check or money order in the amount of $9.95 is
enclosed for the guide, Article Writing: The Best Job
in the World.  I understand that I can examine the
guide for 7-days at your risk.  If I decide to keep
the guide, I will owe nothing more.  If I return it
within 7-days, you are to refund my $9.95.

  ☐ I'd like to see the first part of the guide...as
a sample...before ordering the rest of it.  My check,
cash, or money order for $2 is enclosed.

Name (please print)

Address

City, State, Zip
```

Order Form

spellings. Customers often fill in the order form too quickly and will not print their names unless they are requested to do so.

At the top of my order form, I use the following statement to verify exactly what is being ordered: "Yes. Please send me my copy of *The Sure Way to Stop Smoking*. I understand that I will pay only $9.95." A verification like this is a good idea because it makes ordering easier.

Below the customer's city, state, country, and zip code, many order forms have the words "check—cash—money order," with spaces after each. Customers check which payment method they are using.

Below the method of payment I usually indicate how the item will be mailed or shipped to the customer. So the last line of my order form reads: "Mailed via third-class mail. Please allow time for delivery. You may use this order form to send this item as a gift." It's a good idea to suggest to customers that the form can be used to send the product as a gift. Many mail-order customers will buy more than one item and send them to friends or relatives. This is especially true around the Christmas season.

Quite a few mail-order firms use a simple business reply card. This can be postcard size or the size of a business envelope. I've seen a lot of reply cards, and the simple ones seem to work best. Many say something like this at the top: "Enroll Me Today," or "Mailing Order Label," or "This Offer Is Guaranteed." It's not necessary to say anything at the top of the card. Many reply cards just have dotted lines for the name and address, a checkoff box for what's being ordered, and the means of payment. A number of experienced mail-order operators claim that simple postcard-sized reply cards and business reply envelopes pull far more orders than elaborate, wordy order forms. On the other hand, there are those in the mail-order field who believe that the order form should look as businesslike and important as possible. I advise you to try both kinds. Use a simple postcard-sized reply card for one of your offers and a more elaborate order form for another item. You'll soon discover what works best for you.

Another type of order form that pulled well for me was one I designed myself. I used a full 8½ × 11 sheet of paper. I filled three-quarters of the page with a list of specific benefits of the product. The bottom quarter was used for the order form. I had this full-page order form printed on pink paper, and it's still pulling for me today.

A surefire way to pick a good order form to use for your own products and offers is to answer a number of ads that offer free details. In several months you'll have plenty of mail. Go through each direct-mail offer and take out the order forms. Study each one carefully. You can then decide which type of order form you like best and feel would work for you. Style your own order form in a similar way. This method works and will help you to come up with an order form that will generate profits for you.

THE CIRCULAR

Many authorities in mail order agree that the circular is an important part of any direct-mail package you send out. The circular runs a close second to the sales letter in influencing prospects to buy a mail-order offer. A circular is usually a one- or two-color 8½ × 11 sheet of paper printed on one or both sides. The circular supports your sales letter. You might think of it as extra selling ammunition or bait used to land a prospect. Important information about your product or service not included in your sales letter may be presented in the circular. In this age of consumer doubt and skepticism about many products and services, a circular enables you to back up your offer with extra reasons why a prospect should buy. You can give a lot of details about your offer in a circular and use it to prove your case.

Many newcomers to mail order believe that the circular is not read, and also not practical to plan, print, or mail. But more prospects than you might suspect will at least glance at an attractive circular. Once prospects become interested in an offer through a sales letter, they may then read a circular for more proof of product value.

Circulars are the place for testimonials about your product or offer.

THIS SYSTEM FOR CREATING ALL KINDS OF PROFITABLE IDEAS HAS WORKED FOR ME FOR YEARS. IT IS BRINGING OTHERS A SECOND INCOME, AND I KNOW IT CAN ALSO PUT YOU IN THE IDEA BUSINESS FAST.
Here are QUOTES from some of the many letters in my files accepting ideas I have created FOR CASH: (Copies of these letters and checks received sent on request)
CANADA: (Greeting Card Company) "Enclosed is our check in the amount of $25.00 in payment for your anniversary card idea numbered S-9903-1."
CALIFORNIA: (Security Corp.) "Enclosed you will find our check for $96.00."
VIRGINIA: (Advertising Co.) "Here is our check for the two ads. We thank you for these two excellent submissions."
NEW YORK CITY: "I will pay $65 for the story and $25 for the British psychiatrist idea." (newspaper)
TELEGRAM FROM CANADA: (Magazine) "All material received accepted."
CALIFORNIA SYNDICATE: "I plan to use the story on Gable."
NEW YORK CITY (Syndicate) "Collection report and check for $79.28 for ideas--stories sold to markets in Japan and Mexico."
AUSTRALIA: (News-Sunday Mag.) $56.00 for stories.
FLORIDA (Insurance Company) "Enclosed is our check for $90 for your article."
CHICAGO: "We are buying both your ideas. A check will follow."

ONE DAY'S MAIL ALONE...LAST WEEK... BROUGHT ME 16 IDEA ACCEPTANCES FROM ONE MARKET ALONE. I WANT THE SAME THING TO HAPPEN TO YOU.
SEND THE PINK ORDER FORM TODAY!

Circular

After you've been in mail order a while, you may occasionally receive letters or notes from satisfied customers. These comments are testimonials on the quality and value of your offers. You can use these testimonials and pictures of those who made them in your circulars. Later, you can contact customers directly and request their reactions to your offers.

Photographs of your product can be effective in influencing prospects to buy. The use of a photograph does make a circular more costly to print, but the extra pulling power of a photograph is worth the expense. If there's any way to illustrate the benefits of your offer, then depict these benefits in your circular. It may be an old cliché, but "a picture is still worth a thousand words."

Some direct-mail users try to save money by using typewritten circulars. But when you plan to use a circular to help sell an offer, it's wiser to stick with typeset circulars. Remember: Prospects will judge your company and offer by the appearance of your circular and sales letter. The content of the offer is most important, but the general appearance does make an impression. The neater and more professional-looking your circulars are the better. If you have a word processor and high-quality printer, you can achieve this professional look without having to pay for typesetting.

The question of printing on one or both sides of the circular brings a mixed reaction. Many mail-order operators feel that one side is enough and that there's no guarantee that a prospect is going to read both sides. So some direct-mail veterans try to get everything on one side. Other operators, however, feel that if you can make both sides equally impressive, attractive, and inviting, you will have a definite sales advantage over the one-sided circular. Many circulars, for example, use both sides to present questions and answers about an offer. By using both sides a circular can tell dramatic stories about an offer using elaborate designs, illustrations, sketches, and layouts.

The most effective circulars use an attention-getting headline at the top of the page. A strong headline is often the first thing prospects see when they look at a circular. The strength of the headline may determine whether a prospect decides to read on or not. So try to come up with a real attention grabber. Then your circular won't be ignored.

Your company name and address should be on the circular. The elements of a direct-mail package will frequently get separated and possibly misplaced by prospects. If prospects lose your sales letter, they may sill have your circular. And if your name and address is on it, you won't miss out on an order.

One circular that works well for me is an 8½ × 11 sheet of canary yellow paper printed in black ink on both sides. My company name and address are at the top of one side and also on a detachable coupon at the bottom of the reverse side. The circular has a good headline and layout, but there are no pictures or sketches. I know this circular has selling power because many customers made comments referring to product points and benefits cited in the circular.

You should experiment with different kinds of circulars. Some will work better than others. As your mailbox fills up with various mail-order offers, collect the circulars and keep them in a file so that you can study them as time allows. Use the circulars you like best as a guide when planning your own.

THE REPLY ENVELOPE

In every direct-mail offer you send out, be certain to include a reply envelope (often called a business return envelope). This sounds like an easy thing to remember, and certainly a logical one, but newcomers to mail order sometimes forget to enclose one. Each and every prospect you send a sales letter, circular, and order form to should receive a reply envelope. The whole purpose of your sales letter and circular is to make a prospect send you an immediate order. The order form you enclose makes it easy to order. But if no reply envelope is provided, prospects may forget the whole thing. It's frustrating to look for a reply envelope in a direct-mail package and not find one. When prospects decide to send you an order, they expect to use an envelope that you provide. Few people will take the time and trouble of addressing their own. So be sure to have plenty prepared when you start your mail-order business. Professional-looking ones are best to use. But until you're able to get professionally printed reply envelopes, even envelopes that you've addressed yourself are better than none at all. You're bound to lose a lot of orders—and money—by not enclosing one.

Some mail-order operators use a standard-sized reply envelope. Other operators prefer the long business reply envelope like the kind used for most business purposes. The smaller envelope is cheaper to obtain but not as businesslike. I use the long business reply envelope. In the upper left-hand corner I have three dotted-line spaces printed after the word "From." My company name and address are printed in the center of the envelope. For most of my offers I use black ink on white. A lot of mail-order operators claim that color envelopes usually outpull white ones. I suggest that you test both kinds, as I did.

How many reply envelopes you'll need depends on how much direct mail you plan to send out. I had several thousand envelopes printed when I first started my company and they were used up fast. You can also use reply envelopes when responding to requests for more details from the inquiry and follow-up ads you run.

There are mixed feelings on whether a direct-mail user should supply the postage stamps for return envelopes. Many direct-mail operators claim that by providing stamps they can increase orders considerably; other operators feel the extra postage expense is not justified, and that prospects will use their own stamps if they really want to buy. You might wait until you're more established in your business before supplying return envelope stamps. Try mailing some with stamps and some without stamps to see what kind of results you get.

THE VISUAL EFFECT OF DIRECT MAIL

The use of color in direct mail can definitely increase the number of orders you receive. Prospects everywhere like and respond to colors. Using color means a higher printing expense, but the extra orders you receive make it worthwhile.

Have you ever watched a color television set for several weeks, and then switched to a plain black and white set? The contrast is striking. Millions of us everywhere have become used to color television; we take it for granted and certainly prefer it to black and white. The same is true of color in direct mail. Colors are inviting to the eye when prospects first open their direct-mail envelopes. A sales letter and circular are more appealing to read if printed in bright, attractive colors. This is not to say that you absolutely must use color in your direct-mail offers. You may not be able to afford the extra printing expense. Until you've gained some experience in direct mail, then, you may prefer to use black and white—but keep the idea of using color in the back of your mind. As your business develops, sooner or later you'll want to use some color in your sales letters, circulars, and order forms.

It's true of course that the use of color is no guarantee that a particular product or offer will do well. It's always the offer itself that counts. But the use of color does add a visual incentive to buy.

When people glance through their mail, they're usually first attracted to color envelopes. A good example is the envelope sent out by the American Song Festival for its annual competition. The name and address of the festival appear in red, white, and blue on the upper left corner of the envelope. So an appealing patriotic visual effect is achieved.

The mail-order departments of many book publishers use color effectively in their direct mailings. One publisher's sales letter I received is printed in black and green ink on white paper. It is very eye-catching. Another letter of this type is printed in black ink on white paper, with key lines underlined in blue. The headline and closing of this letter are also blue.

Sales letters and business reply envelopes come in all styles and color combinations. One popular color combination used is red and black ink on white paper. The effect is striking. The use of red ink in combination with other colors has become increasingly popular. One sales letter of mine printed in blue ink on white paper did particularly well. So it isn't always necessary to have two or three colors. It's well known in mail order that blue ink (and shades of blue paper) generally pull well with both male and female prospects, though men respond somewhat better to blue. Pink and canary yellow often bring a good response from women. Your printer can suggest ideas and color schemes to create an unusual effect.

Many effective order forms use blue or green ink on a white background, or black ink on a gold background. An order form I've seen recently uses three colors. The order form is the exact size of a check and even looks like a check. The copy of the form is printed in black and red ink on a blue-green background. This is one of the best-looking order forms I've seen. It will no doubt influence many prospects to send in an order.

When you're ready to use color in your direct mailings, here are some color combinations to consider. These have worked well in my own business and also for many other mail-order operators:

1. Blue ink on white paper
2. Blue and black ink on white paper
3. Red and black ink on white paper
4. Blue or black ink on canary yellow paper
5. Black ink on pink paper (has strong appeal for women)
6. Black, green, and red in any combination of ink or paper

Don't feel like you have to use color in your mailings to get orders. Color can often increase the response, but one of my first sales letters was printed in black ink on white paper and sold very well. Even if everything in your direct-mail package consists of black ink on white paper, it can still bring in orders. But if you can afford to use color, you should do so. Even one color will bring you better results. Try sending out one mailing consisting of all black ink on white paper and another mailing using color, and then compare the results. This test may convince you that the extra expense for color is justified. But generally, most prospects are interested in your offer—not how much color is evident. So don't let the lack of color keep you from using direct mail.

There are other kinds of visual effects used in direct mail. Some of them include the following:

1. Sketches and illustrations of the product or service in use
2. Photographs of satisfied customers
3. Photographs of the mail-order operators themselves used in a circular to influence prospects to buy
4. Cartoon-type panels and balloons and humorous-looking figures using the product
5. Occult or mystical-looking mazes, sketches, symbols, and designs used to sell occult products

Ask yourself how more visual effects can be applied to your direct-mail package. By keeping all of the visual possibilities in mind you're sure to come up with some good ideas. You don't have to be a commercial artist to add flavor and appeal to your mailings. You probably at least have the ability to draw a simple sketch showing your product in action. You can certainly draw stars, brackets, mystical circles, dollar signs, and other simple effects. Just keep thinking about what might make your letter come alive, add appeal to your order form, liven up your circular, and make the outside envelope more effective.

For my offer of a music guidance report, I used drawings of musical notes in my sales letter and circular. The notes added a lot of style to my offer and made the entire product stand out in the minds of prospects. You can come up with good visual effects like mine if you do some creative thinking. See what's being done in other direct mailings and experiment with your own ideas.

Visual effects can increase your direct-mail profits. Remember: The visual effects you use in your direct mailings can make your offers stand out from the competition. So use visual effects for extra selling power.

13

Latest Direct-Mail Ideas

Direct-mail opportunities in the 1990s are both dynamic and overwhelming. Millions of people are out of work due to an economic recession that magnate Donald Trump calls "a depression, not a recession." These out-of-work people are searching for new ways to make money, to start a business of their own, to launch a service, to pay off their debts, and to solve their problems. In short, it's a great time to get into direct mail—provided you have something of real value and quality that will help buyers in a specific way.

Most people never actually start a business, but they are interested in considering the idea, reading about possible ventures, and dreaming of the possibilities. They like to read about how others did it. This huge market is always there, and more so in bad economic periods. If you sell items that help people cope with hard times, they'll buy from you again and again, in good times as well.

THE GILLETTE COMPANY'S DIRECT-MAIL BOOM

Some companies are discovering the power of direct mail. After the initial success of Gillette's Sensor Razor, the company was eager to keep the momentum going.

So what did Gillette do? In four words: *They discovered direct mail.* The company mailed coupons worth $2.00 or $3.00 (off the almost $4.00 razor) to five million men. The coupons had address labels on the reverse side, and this enabled Gillette to set up a customer list. "The real sales come later with blade repurchases," according to a Gillette marketing executive.

TEN WAYS TO UPGRADE YOUR
DIRECT-MAIL PROFITS

1. Gear your direct-mail offers closely to the needs and interests of prospects. Jobs and job information, for example, are what many buyers want during bad economic periods.

2. People are always trying to cut back on their expenses. There remains a strong interest in products like the following:

    Information guides on saving money

    Money sources—where to borrow from

    Any and all materials on generating money

    Moonlighting ideas

    Guidelines, information, and assistance for debt management. Buyers want proven plans that really work.

3. Think about products or services that will help parents. One current offering is a list of 14 ways to help parents renew the lives of their children and get them headed in the right direction. This direct-mail product has great potential.

4. If you can, accept credit card orders via a toll-free 800 number. It will definitely increase the number of orders you receive. Many buyers prefer to purchase items with their credit cards so they can pay the bill later.

5. If your offer is similar to others, add something to give it a competitive edge. You might lower the price, or make your product more efficient, useful, and practical than competing ones.

6. Determine who the best customers on your ongoing list are and continue mailing to them. Those repeat customers who buy from you again and again are your best asset. Keep presenting them with additional opportunities to buy from you. Once you acquire a regular customer base, your profits can increase dramatically.

7. Remember: Direct mail can be effectively used to sell a service as well as a product. Some companies use direct mail for both.

8. Increase the drawing power of your direct-mail offers by giving your prospects the choice of paying later. Do this by simply adding a "bill me later" box on the order form.

9. An excellent way to keep sales brisk, even during economic recessions, is to offer your customers the option of an Easy Payment Plan. This means more paperwork and record keeping for you, but it's well worth it to get those additional orders.

10. Few businesses realize the power and profitability of direct mail. Many businesses haven't even considered it. This will undoubtedly change as more and more direct-mail success stories emerge.

   The word is being spread that direct mail works. More companies in the coming years are likely to jump on the bandwagon. Business-to-business direct mail already generates over $120 million a year. I expect this to be much higher by the turn of the century.

14

Mailing Lists

INEXPENSIVE VERSUS EXPENSIVE NAME LISTS

Any experience with direct-mail advertising will make you aware of the importance of mailing lists. Quality lists are absolutely crucial for success.

There are many mailing lists, and you simply cannot be sure if they are reliable or not unless you investigate them before ordering. If you go ahead and order 5,000 names without first getting all the facts about the list, you may be sorry.

One problem with cheaper lists, often called "bargain" lists, is that deadwood names have not been taken out recently. This could mean that 60 to 80 percent of the names on such lists are not deliverable, so you would obviously waste money, postage, and effort using them.

To avoid an unsuccessful outcome, always ask the list owners how long it's been since the list has been purged of useless, deadwood names.

Even some of the medium-priced and expensive mailing lists are of poor quality. I've been burned a number of times by poor lists that were described as "top quality" or "fresh hot names."

In my own experience, I've found that some expensive lists are not as good as the more moderate or even cheaper priced ones. There's no rule on this. You should try all three types to determine which ones will work best for you.

OTHER FACTORS TO CONSIDER

Before purchasing a list you should consider a number of factors:

- The nature of your product or service
- The specific market you're trying to reach
- How many names you're renting
- The type of product-service items those on a particular list buy
- The reputation of the mailing list company.

Ask yourself these questions:

- Is the age of those on the list right for your offer?
- Are refunds offered by the list company you're considering? Some list companies give you 10 or 20 new names for every undeliverable name on a list you purchase.
- Is the list up to date? Some lists have many incorrect addresses. This wastes your time, effort, and postage.
- How receptive will those on the list be to the type of offer (product, item, or service) you send them? If they've been interested in similar offers in the past, that's a good sign.
- Does the Better Business Bureau (in the area where the list company is located) have any negative information about that company?

In my other book on mail order, *How to Make Money in Mail Order* (John Wiley and Sons, Inc., 605 Third Avenue, New York, NY 10158), you'll find almost seven pages of mailing list companies with their addresses and key facts about the lists they offer.

Hugo Dunhill Mailing Lists, Inc. (630 Third Avenue, New York, NY 10017, toll free: 800-223-6454) provides an up-to-date Mailing List Catalog, which is reportedly the world's largest. In this catalog you'll find mailing lists targeting a wide variety of fields, including accounting, clubs, education, executives (by function, or in international firms), government, computers, communications, real estate, religion, recreation, aviation, law, medicine, libraries, and more.

Don't limit yourself to one list. Test others periodically and investigate the mailing lists you hear or read about. Try to find several companies that provide responsive, quality names. Then you can divide your list business among them or go with a single company. It's up to you.

The point is that it's well worth your time and effort to find strong pulling lists that will increase your orders and your profits.

15

The Power of Direct-Mail Advertising

The key to success and profit in direct-mail advertising requires the right product or service, the right sales letter, the right direct-mail package (including sales letter, circular, order form, and return envelope), and the right mailing list.

My own feeling is that the sales letter you send is the single most important item in your entire direct mail package. If your sales letter really hooks the prospect, and persuades that person to make a buying decision, you're going to receive an order. The mailing list you use, the circular, the order form, and the return envelope are all important, but your sales letter is the key.

I've watched a number of prospects open direct-mail offers. The majority of them put everything aside except the sales letter. If it hooks and holds their attention, they send in an order. Others, however, will look at the circular first (if one is enclosed)—especially if it's a multicolor sheet with a handsome picture.

Sooner or later you should try direct-mail advertising. That's where big money profits are waiting, but you must know what you're doing. First create your direct-mail package. Then get the best selected mailing list you can find, without spending a fortune. Test it with a mailing to 5,000 or 10,000 names. If your results show you have a winner, you can increase the size of your mailings.

One trouble with direct mail is that it's very time-consuming. It takes money and time to prepare large mailings to 10,000 or 20,000 names. Some firms mail to hundreds of thousands and even millions of names.

Think of the postage bills for such huge mailings. This is why many wait until they have assistants before moving into this branch of the business. Remember: There are companies that specialize in this area. They will do the mailings for you—to as many names as you want—for a price.

To give you an idea of the success some companies are achieving, or may achieve, with direct mail, consider the following:

- A publishing company interested in children's education launched a product called *Success: Guiding Your Child to Learning.* Their ad is a comic strip directed to and mailed to parents. It's an interesting idea that may be very profitable.
- Former Senator S. I. Hayakawa has used direct-mail advertising for years to promote his U.S. English program. One-hundred-dollar contributors have been invited (in sales letters) to spend $250.00 to $5,000.00 a year to join the "U.S. English Inner Circle."
- I already mentioned the Gillette Company's successful use of direct mail to maintain sales momentum for its Sensor Razor product.
- Omaha Steaks continues to do well with direct mail, sending out attractive literature about its product. Satisfied customers have dealt with this company for years and continue to send orders by mail.
- More and more book publishers are jumping on the direct-mail bandwagon. They've discovered that using direct mail increases their sales and overall profits.

Part IV

PRACTICAL
CONSIDERATIONS

SUCCESS STORY: John Bear

John Bear got into the mail-order business with one good idea: He decided to publish and advertise a report on how to get a college degree by mail. One of John's early ads cost him $120.00 and returned a gross of $7,000.00. His net profit turned out to be about $5,000.00. Delighted with his success in mail order, Bear made some changes in his life: He left his job in Chicago and moved to northern California. He then began to run his ad in over 30 leading mail-order publications and has enjoyed a handsome retirement income from his huge profits.

16

Marketing on a Global Basis

Keeping up with mail-order products and services in America takes enough time, but now you're faced with an even greater challenge (read opportunity): marketing on a global basis. The amazing political changes of late have produced a new global picture. The Soviet Union as we once knew it is gone. Germany is reunited. U.S. marketing executives are opening company branches in Europe, and moving there themselves to be on the scene.

There will soon be a single European market. American companies that have anticipated this will be ready when this vast marketplace opens up. This one European market will offer an incredible 344 million consumers, which is 50 percent more than in America. And that figure is bound to increase.

Think of the overwhelming opportunity. By staying informed of what is happening in Europe, you'll know which products and services are being sold successfully overseas. Then it becomes possible to contact the owners of these hit products, and ask for exclusive rights to sell them in America.

You may not wish to offer a successful European product here in the States. You may be too busy selling your own product(s) by mail. But a product that clicks in Europe could also do very well here. The decision is yours. It's nice to have a choice.

An excellent way to watch for hot product offerings overseas is to read foreign trade journals like *Advertising Age*'s *Euromarketing Newsletter*.

Attorney Klaus Burmeister specializes in European Community-U.S. transactions and has written that "a key basic of the new European Community is the free movement of goods, but they must be produced within the European Community or legally imported and circulated anywhere in the Community."

Obviously, if American mail-order firms, as well as other U.S. companies, want to do business in the European Community, they will have to meet the competition—and the 19 countries comprising the European Community will be very competitive. According to the EC Commission, "A strong competition policy is essential in order to maintain the unity of the internal market."

If you're interested in selling products from other countries in the States, you should write to foreign consulate offices to express your interest. These offices can also help if you wish to offer your own products in their countries. Please keep in mind that the following addresses are subject to change:

Britain
845 Third Avenue
New York, NY
10022

Italy
690 Park Avenue
New York, NY
10021

The Republic of Ireland
580 Fifth Avenue
New York, NY
10020

Denmark
280 Park Avenue
New York, NY
10017

France
40 West 57th Street
New York, NY
10019

Germany
460 Park Avenue
New York, NY
10022

Austria
31 East 69th Street
New York, NY
10021

Israel
800 Second Avenue
New York, NY
10017

Switzerland
444 Madison Avenue
New York, NY
10017

Japan
280 Park Avenue
New York, NY
10017

Norway
800 Third Avenue
New York, NY
10004

Mexico
8 East 41 Street
New York, NY
10017

United Kingdom
150 East 58th Street
New York, NY
10022

To help you decide if marketing your mail-order product(s) overseas is the right way to go, here are some key questions you should ask yourself:

1. Is your product right for the overseas country you're considering?
2. Are similar products now being sold there? If so, is there too much competition?
3. Can you do the necessary advertising to reach the right market?
4. Can you afford the increased cost of advertising? The difference between British pounds and U.S. dollars, for example, will mean that your cost for ads in Britain will most likely be higher. The rate between pounds and dollars changes daily.
5. Can you manage the higher postage tab in sending mail to prospects in other countries? This is assuming you use direct mail. Filling orders will also cost more.

On the other hand, think of the millions of prospects in other countries you have an opportunity to reach. It's a huge market of 344 million consumers. There's no question that many American companies will get their share of it. You could share in this bonanza too. You might do very well. Much depends on the nature of the product you offer and whether your profit rate, in doing business overseas, will be high enough after all advertising and mailing costs are met.

My advice is to go slow at first. Gather the information you need and see if your profit would be enough, after all costs are absorbed. Test classified ads and several thousand names (if using direct mail). If results are good, then you can gradually increase your advertising.

Always test first on a small scale before investing too much of your money. If there's one wise, strategic word for the mail-order business, it's "test." Testing can save you a lot of money and trouble. It will indicate whether you have a winning offer or not. Don't proceed any farther unless your tests give you the go signal.

17

Mail-Order Products, Services, and Businesses in Demand Overseas

Many American companies have learned they can save a bundle in research and development money by tracking new, successful products overseas and then introducing them into the States, often as brand new products or repackaged versions of the originals.

The obvious advantage of this strategy is in having a ready-made product in which most of the problems have already been solved. The mortality rate for new products is about 80 percent, so developing something from scratch is expensive and risky.

You should make yourself aware of some mail-order products that are being offered overseas. You might decide to offer something similar here in the States. You'll notice that some items seem to sell well everywhere.

The following products may be used as springboards to other new items or variations:

- Printing by mail (good repeat business item)
- Mail-order books (sold to customers, dealers, and discount stores)
- Rainy weather windshield cleaners
- Crumpets (British flat cakes)

- Computer matching service (some even find suitable running partners for joggers)
- Executive search services (This industry is growing quickly—especially in Japan.)
- Curved bath brushes (curved 180 degrees so you can wash your back without twisting your neck)
- Telephone auto dialer
- Talking toys (talking trucks, trains, airplanes, and others)
- Electronic mosquito repeller
- Pet foods
- Food in tubes (large toothpaste-like tubes with screw tops to store food in after cans have been opened—available in Europe)
- All kinds of correspondence courses (doll-making, dress-knitting, business skills, handwriting improvement, investing, and more)
- Stuffed dolls and animals
- Clever new types of coin banks
- Health products
- Environmental products (soaps, shampoos, water/air filters, and many more)
- Dieting materials
- Cigarette timer (a gadget rings a bell when the owner has smoked a set daily allowance of cigarettes)
- Future forecasting materials (crystal balls, tarot cards, and more)
- Overseas employment handbooks, guides, and directories
- Stain removers
- Catalog research service
- Coin-investing course
- Plastic business signs
- Wooden necklaces
- Spelling and grammar improvement aids
- Spare bed (that can be taken anywhere)
- Photos reproduced on plates
- Rubber stamps
- Name bracelets
- Baseball caps
- Talking balloons and watches

- Novelty placemats
- Foot and back massagers
- Mini first aid kits
- Hot tubs and saunas
- Computer software and books
- Fruit and floral decorations
- Clock-making kits
- Solar devices
- Movie posters
- Slogan buttons
- Gourmet foods
- Scarves and gloves
- Designer glasses
- Plug-in-cars
- Fingernail and toenail lotion
- Minicomputers
- Birthstone watches
- Reminder products (to take medicine)
- Ski goggles
- Creams and lotions to restore youthful appearance and reduce wrinkles
- Golf umbrellas
- Nail-grooming set
- Magnetic paperclip holders
- Golf tee bags

To give you an idea of what types of business ventures are being offered overseas, some of the current franchise opportunities in the United Kingdom (for purchase) are:

- Laser personalized stationery
- Convenience store chains
- Sports/leisure (selling top brand name sports and leisure clothing and footwear)
- Mobile car valeting franchise
- Personalized children's and adult books

- Training for opening your own real estate agency (selling homes and businesses)
- Co-op direct mail
- Disaster restoration (surfaces and items restored after smoke, fire, or flood damage)
- Coffee distributorships
- Fashion, gift, and jewelry business
- Legal services marketing business
- Window blinds
- Kitchen showroom franchises

18

Products That Will Sell In Japan

In a recent poll conducted by the *Wall Street Journal,* NBC News, and *Nippon News,* an interesting key question was asked: Which nation do Americans and Japanese believe is stronger in technology and science at this point in time? A solid majority of 63 percent of Americans polled believed Japan was stronger, while 32 percent thought America was stronger. But 63 percent of Japanese believed the United States was stronger, and only 18 percent thought Japan was stronger.

It's reassuring to know that a *Business Week*/Harris poll found that "only 21 percent of the Japanese think America has begun a process of irreversible decline." Given that American products still have clout in Japan, think well about offering your products and mail-order items there. If your offers match their interests and needs, you might do very well indeed. Some guidelines may help you decide.

Education is very important in Japan, so education-related products might do well. Japan's college-age students might respond enthusiastically to information materials on how to get accepted in M.B.A. (Master of Business Administration) programs at top American colleges and business schools. You could prepare printed material, or offer a tape cassette. This idea could be a big money maker for you, assuming you could get your hands on a mailing list of Japanese students planning to study for M.B.A. degrees in the States. If this interests you, I suggest you write the Japan foreign consulate office.

Due to the overcrowded conditions in their country the Japanese like wide open spaces and enjoy vacations that offer plenty of room. Perhaps you now have a product that meets, or is related, to this love of wide open spaces. If not, maybe you could develop something along these lines, such as a vacation guide or information on travel bargains.

Despite the fact that the work ethic is still quite strong in Japan, there seems to be a developing trend toward taking life easier. Many more Japanese are now in the mood to enjoy the rewards and benefits of their hard work.

Japanese workers, and executives, worked unbelievable schedules for years, but it cost the health and even lives of many. Some executives would leave in the early morning and not return home until eleven o'clock or midnight each evening seven days a week. A number of these workaholics have simply dropped dead, and this has influenced more people in the country to realize that the time has come to enjoy some of the fruits of their hard work.

Do you now have a product or offer that would appeal to the present Japanese interest in

- More leisure time
- Increased interest in sports (like learning to play golf)
- Pursuit of the good life
- Joining country clubs
- Travel
- Dressing well
- Buying merchandise with brand names

An increasing number of Japanese see themselves as members of the successful middle class. It's difficult to change from their six- to seven-day workweek, but more are trying to do so. One sign of this change is that since mid-1991, their banks and stock market exchange are now closed on Saturdays.

To an increasing degree, the Japanese are becoming more like American consumers. If this trend continues, Japanese consumers should respond positively to products and items you are now offering buyers here in the States. You can certainly see from this how a whole new market is emerging, a market responsive to a vast array of American products and services.

So what you should do is compare your present existing product offers with the seven enjoyment goals previously listed. Then ask yourself a question: Is there a good match or mix?

Do you now offer anything that relates to the Japanese market? If not, perhaps you can develop an offer and test it with magazine ads or with direct-mail offers you send to prospects in Japan. Contact the Japan foreign consulate office for up-to-date information on postage, customs, and the like.

While new entertainment-related items offered in Japan should do especially well, there are also many stand-by mail-order items that have previously sold well and are still bringing in orders. Here are some examples:

- Correspondence courses on hobbies and crafts
- Air pumps (pumps up car or bike tires in seconds)
- Electronic light switches
- Coin and cigarette banks
- Good luck charms
- New teaching systems
- Telescope and microscope combination
- Money-making information
- Dolls
- A wide variety of novelty products
- Games
- Rings
- Diet cakes (sold by a franchise system)

One service item presently in demand in Japan is called the Chartered Financial Analyst designation. This is a professional certification program run by the Association for Investment Management and Research in Charlottesville, Virginia. Japanese interest in this accreditation program has been exploding. The program includes a set of tough examinations and three years of independent study.

19

Filling Orders

ACKNOWLEDGING ORDERS

One aspect of running your mail-order business is acknowledging orders. There are two views on this. Some mail-order operators are convinced that sending acknowledgments to customers is a must for success. Other operators believe that this practice is an unnecessary extra expense. The choice is yours.

I usually send acknowledgments myself. Here are some sound reasons for doing so:

1. It's good business. It instills good will and confidence in the customer for you and your company.
2. It makes customers feel that they are important and valuable to your company.
3. It shows your appreciation for a customer's order.
4. It encourages repeat business.
5. It stimulates customer loyalty.
6. It assures customers that their orders have arrived safely.

Remember: An acknowledgment is your written confirmation to a customer that an order has been received. People often worry about their mail being lost. Acknowledgments do a lot to erase this worry and help to upgrade the reputation of the mail-order industry. Therefore, acknowledgments are worth the extra time and money and can aid you in building a successful mail-order company.

There are two types of acknowledgments—the form and the personal letter. Both types state that the order has been received and will be filled as quickly as possible. Many mail-order operators prefer the personal letter because it has warmth and shows a greater feeling of appreciation to the customer. Sending a form acknowledgment, however, is better than none at all. When you begin to receive hundreds of orders daily, you may be forced to use a form acknowledgment. (Although if you own a word processor, a "personal" letter will take only seconds to adapt from a template.)

FILLING ORDERS

You would think that all mail-order firms would automatically treat their orders with tender loving care. This just isn't true. There are many companies that react to orders with an uncaring and unprofessional attitude. Orders are the lifeblood of a mail-order business. Make it a rule to handle orders with respect and efficiency.

One mail-order company advertises about the speed with which it fills orders. But some of their customers have waited six to eight weeks to receive small orders. Many mail-order printing firms take far too long to fill orders. In most of these cases, no explanation for the delay is given.

Why are orders treated so carelessly by some companies? One reason is inefficiency. People make errors. They misplace orders or let them accumulate unopened. At times, some of these companies only have a skeleton crew filling orders with little supervision. When you need help in your business, try to hire dependable people who will fill orders promptly.

Customers who have had bad experiences with mail-order firms often spread the word and sometimes contact postal authorities. Some mail-order companies have lost their right to do business by mail for delaying or not filling orders and for refusing to return a customer's money on a guaranteed offer.

Many people believe that service is a thing of the past. This is one reason why more and more people choose to do business by mail. So mail-order firms that fill orders carelessly hurt the firms that fill orders responsibly and professionally. Reputable mail-order companies fill their orders within 24 hours or at most a few days.

Some of the larger mail-order companies have poor service due to poor management. An order I sent to a mail-order printing company is a good example. I ordered 1,000 business reply envelopes and paid extra to have lines printed on the reverse side. I received this order, and later sent another order for the same kind of envelope. This time I received no order and got instead a note from the firm stating that they do not fill orders with printing on the reverse side of the envelope. I was amazed at this reply because the firm had filled the same order before. I wondered if some skeleton crew member had received my order, not felt like bothering with it, and sent me the note stating that my order couldn't be filled. What a way to do business! I never ordered from this firm again.

The average businessperson used to take pride in seeing that all mail received a courteous, professional, and prompt reply. This is no longer true in many cases. As a test, I once sent a professionally typed letter on my business letterhead to 250 mail-order companies. A stamped return envelope was enclosed with half of the letters, but I received only seven replies. This test is a good indication of how indifferent some mail-order companies have become. As you build your own mail-order business, strive to answer all orders and requests in a careful, professional, and prompt manner. By doing this, you will build a solid reputation of integrity and your mail-order company will grow and prosper.

KEEPING ACCURATE RECORDS

The necessary records in mail order are simple and easy to maintain. When I launched my mail-order firm I got a three-ring notebook and some paper with 12 lines across it. This allowed me room for eight divisions (or headings) on each sheet. I recommend that you do the same or use a similar system. Computer spreadsheet programs work very well for this, since information can be stored and later sorted to create your own mailing list.

I wrote the following headings across the top of each page:

Date Order Received
Name of Customer
Address of Customer
Amount Enclosed
Method of Payment
Date Order Filled
Postage Cost
Key Code

| Publication Ad Run in _____ | | | Charge Per Word or Line _____ | | | | | |
| Address _____ | | | Heading of Ad _____ | | | | | |
Date Received	Name of Customer	Address of Customer	Amount Enclosed	Method of Payment	Date Order Filled		Key Code	Postage Cost

Record Keeping Chart

Date Order Received

It's important to know the exact date on which you received an order or a request for details. The date should be the first division in your record-keeping system. I find that it's best to record the date of every order or inquiry immediately after opening each day's mail. This way it gets done at once, before anything distracts you. You'll find this information to be useful for income-tax purposes.

Name of Customer

The most vital information of all is the name of each customer who sends you an order or an inquiry. When you record a customer's name in your records, write or type it just as you received it on the order form or envelope. Sometimes you can't be sure of the exact spelling of a customer's name because it is not written clearly. To avoid this, have a line printed on your order form requesting customers to "please print."

Many mail-order operators also type or print the names of their customers on index cards. Each index card is a record of your business with a customer. Each offer that someone buys and the date the order was received should be listed on the index cards. Whether the customer responded directly from an ad, sent in an inquiry, or replied to a direct-mail package should also be listed. I know this sounds like a lot of record-keeping, but I cannot stress enough how important this information is to you. It's as good as money in the bank, for it will enable you to sell to customers repeatedly. And, also, your list of names can be sold to other mail-order operators.

Address of Customer

You should write down the address of each customer on your record sheet and also on your index card. By having the addresses written in two separate places, you will be less likely to lose them. Many mail-order customers have a post office box in their address, so be sure to record the numbers correctly. Double-check each address, and don't forget to include zip codes. Zip codes usually speed up the delivery of your mail. If you are using a computer, be sure to keep a hard copy of your list in case your disk gets damaged.

Amount Enclosed

"Amount enclosed" is that lovely looking column on your record sheet where you record the amount of money sent in by each customer. When you begin to receive your first orders with checks and money orders in them, the full scope of this amazing mail-order business will begin to dawn on you. Even if your first offers are low-priced items, it will be exciting just to open your mail and find money inside. Once this happens, I predict that it will be hard to get you out of mail order.

For requests for more details on your offers you can simply write "inquiry" in the column used for the amount enclosed. Or you can have a separate column on your record sheet headed "Inquiries." This way, each time you receive an inquiry on an offer from a customer, just put a check mark in the inquiry column for that customer's name.

Method of Payment

Did your customer send you a check or a money order? You record this information in the "Method of Payment" column. I advise against using C.O.D. orders because special postal arrangements must be made, and it's not as popular a payment method today as it was in the past. Most customers prefer check, money order, or credit card.

To set up credit card orders, contact the card company and enter into an agreement with them.

Some customers still insist on sending cash, despite the risk. Some orders may be lost if you do not permit cash payments.

Date Order Filled

The date you mail your product, or details on an offer, is recorded in the "Date Order Filled" column. This information is important because it verifies that each order has been mailed.

Postage Cost

The amount of money you spend on postage is recorded in the "Postage Cost" column. You definitely need to keep up with how much money you spend. Postage costs can add up quickly—especially when you're filling hundreds of orders each month.

Key Code

The last column heading on your record sheet should be the key codes. This column will let you know which ads are pulling in the most orders. When the same key keeps appearing in this column, you'll know that the ad it represents is definitely a winner.

This eight-column system is a simple way of keeping records for your mail-order business. You might want to alter this system by using an entire sheet of paper, a special form, a computer spreadsheet, or a file folder for each heading. There are, of course, more elaborate systems you could use. In time, you may develop your own. But the eight-column system will get you started. It has worked well for me and it can work for you.

Other Business Expenses

A good place to keep a record of your other business expenses is on your record sheets in a separate section of your three-ring notebook. The following are examples of column headings for other expenses.

- Date Expense Incurred
- Description
- Advertising Expense
- Printing Expense
- Professional Service Expense

The point is to keep up with your expenses in a way that does not confuse you. Any method that is logical and businesslike is okay. The records you maintain are tangible proof of the money you spend on your business. This can be very important when income-tax time rolls around. Be sure to save receipts to back up your records, too.

20

Mail-Order Fraud

FALSE ADVERTISING

The sad thing about mail-order fraud is that it hurts the honest people in the industry who are offering legitimate products with genuine value. After being cheated once, victims of swindlers may never trust another ad or piece of direct mail they receive. Mail order would be an even richer and larger industry today if all those who've been cheated could be brought back into the buying-by-mail fold.

Along with the majority of honest and enterprising men and women who are attracted to mail order, con artists and swindlers have also found a home. In the United States alone, over 142,000 complaints for mail fraud were received by the Postal Service in 1982. And the number of complaints continues to rise. The following are the main reasons for these complaints:

1. Orders never received
2. Orders half filled but never completed
3. Orders in damaged condition
4. Orders don't work as advertised and are unsatisfactory
5. Money-back refunds not honored

Research conducted by the Federal Trade Commission reveals that over 6,000 companies in the United States do more than $40 billion a year in mail-order sales. And this figure is increasing each year. In the words of Jerome Lamet, the assistant regional commissioner of the FTC's Chicago office, "There isn't a day that goes by that we don't get one or two complaints about mail-order companies."

A man in Illinois was arrested for cheating customers out of $2 million. His product was a $16.95 digital watch, and the ad for it promised a free pocket calculator for every order of two watches. The catch is that nobody ever received a watch, even though thousands of people sent in cash orders. Not one watch or calculator was ever received. Finally, postal authorities stopped all mail to the company. A whopping $1.2 million was eventually traced to various banks. Another $800,000 was stashed in Mexican banks and may never be recovered.

According to postal inspectors, Americans lost $514 million to mail-order fraud in a recent year, and this figure is $119 million more than the year before. False advertising and misrepresented products are filling the bank accounts of swindlers, con artists, and crooks. Beware of "pie-in-the-sky" promises and "riches-beyond-your-wildest-dream" deals.

One mail-order firm sent direct-mail offers that looked like government notices to veterans. Many veterans know that they have some form of burial benefits, but they don't know exactly what they are. So when they read this direct-mail offer concerning burial benefits, they thought it was part of a government program. Consequently, many veterans lost money because of this scheme.

LAND FRAUD

Land sale is a big mail-order business. You'd be surprised how much land is sold by ads and direct mail. Many land sales are entirely ethical and genuine. But a lot of land—entirely worthless—is sold to gullible buyers.

The advertising used in crooked land deals is very misleading, if not false. Many people buy land sight unseen, and that's where the swindle comes in. The direct-mail sales brochure that prospects see describes the land site in beautiful color pictures and exciting copy. There are usually mountains in the background. A town is also near the land. But when mail-order buyers visit the land they've bought, they often discover that the mountains aren't as close to their land as the pictures indicated, the town is farther from their land than advertised, there are few roads to and from the property, and the true value of the land is much less than what they had been led to believe. People from all walks of life have sunk thousands of dollars into half- or full-acre ranchettes, and later find out that the real estate they've bought is almost worthless. Retired people are prime targets for crooked and fraudulent land deals.

One way mail-order land development firms spark the initial interest of prospects is through a free dinner, film, and trip to the site. I once received an invitation in the mail to a free steak dinner and color-film showing of New Mexico land a company was offering. I accepted. I had a fine meal that didn't cost me a cent, watched a very interesting film about the state of New Mexico, and came close to flying out to the site. Many land offers presented in this way are genuine and conducted by ethical companies—but some are not.

A bulletin issued by HUD (U.S. Department of Housing and Urban Development) warns people about mail-order land deals: "A development might be described as 10 miles from Rainbow City without any indication that the 10 miles leads through an impassable swamp and that it is 34 miles via passable roads."

Another misleading ad offers buyers a chance to become a "land baron" for just a few dollars down and $20.00 a month. These potential buyers imagine that they can own a big chunk of land, but the actual dimensions turn out to be more like 50 × 140 feet.

CHAIN LETTERS

There's been a sharp increase in the number and variety of chain letters in the last few years. Postal authorities say that "any chain letter which seeks something of value may be a violation of the federal lottery or mail fraud statutes." If a chain letter seeks to circulate things of no value— such as a recipe—it is entirely legal. Some chain letters are able to operate on the fringe of the law and, even though they are rip-offs, are considered legal. Most chain letter schemes hurt the reputation of the mail-order industry.

A friend of mine once received a typical chain letter. It gave instructions on how to make a lot of money in a few weeks. My friend was advised to send $2.00 to the last name of five listed in the letter, type his own name as the first name on the list, and omit the last name on the list (the one he sent the $2.00 to). He was urged to have 200 to 500 copies of the letter printed and mailed to known mail-order buyers from a rented list. According to the letter, he could receive $10,000 or more by following these directions. So to prove to himself that sending out chain letters is a waste of time and money, he followed the instructions exactly. What was the result? A total zero. He never received one letter or dollar in the mail. There will probably always be gullible people who believe that they can get something for nothing. Don't fall for any of these chain letter schemes. Tear them up pronto whenever you receive them. Never become involved in any kind of chain scheme sent through the mail. It can tarnish your good name and reputation fast and could ruin your future in mail order. Treat your customers the same way you'd like to be treated. Even though you don't see your mail-order customers, you still have a responsibility to deal with them ethically and fairly.

OLD MAIL FRAUDS

People still seem to fall for the same old con deals. Some con deals are modernized or disguised in some way, but they still are rip-offs by mail. Here are several old con deals that are still being used today. Be on the alert for them.

1. Fake invoices for items that were never ordered
2. Phony ads for products that are never shipped
3. Phony work-at-home deals (Some of these are honest offers. But many buyers are cheated through an "easy money" approach.)
4. Phony contests that hook "winners" into buying expensive products
5. Pyramid schemes
6. Nonexistent correspondence schools (Buyers are offered training for high-paying and glamorous jobs that don't exist.)

Check over this list when you are suspicious of an offer. Many con artists can be put out of business if you report these crooked deals to your local postmaster. Most mail-order firms are honest and ethical, but the bad ones have to be eliminated.

A spokesman for the Postal Service's consumer protection office says, "A lot of people have the attitude that if the ad is published, then they can trust the product. But we have no authority to check out a product in advance. We move in only when we get complaints about something." So to a surprising degree, the mail-order industry is a business of trust. Mail-order buyers trust that their orders will be shipped promptly and will arrive in good condition. A cash order, in itself, implies a buyer's trust in a mail-order firm.

MAIL-ORDER REGULATIONS

Since the FTC has laid down new regulations, there have been fewer complaints about mail-order firms not sending goods that have been ordered and paid for. Some of these new rules require mail-order firms to do the following:

1. Inform customers within 30 days that their order has been received.
2. Supply customers with a postage-free way to cancel a delayed order (a reply card, for example).
3. Refund a customer's money within 7 business days after receiving a notice of cancellation.

The FTC now has the power to take mail-order companies that violate these laws to court. An injunction can be obtained against any mail-order firm in violation of the regulations. The present penalties for violations range up to $10,000 per day.

21

Mail-Order Millionaires

Through the rest of this century and beyond, prosperous growth is predicted for the mail-order industry. Mail-order profits can be enormous, and you have just as good a chance to get your share of them as anyone else. Over the years, mail-order operators have done well part-time and full-time. Many have become millionaires. I have no way of knowing how well you will do in mail order, but I can assure you that the day you launch your mail-order company you'll be entering a fabulous growth industry. The chance to make more money than you ever dreamed is waiting for you in mail order.

MANY MAIL-ORDER MILLIONAIRES STILL ADVERTISE

Read the leading mail-order publications, and you'll notice that many millionaires still run classified ads. There's a four-star lesson here. Why do individuals who have become millionaires via mail order continue to run classified ads? Because they learned long ago that classified ads will continue to build their invaluable customer list. Most mail-order millionaires owe a lot of their success to classified inquiry and follow-up ads. These ads helped to get their business off the ground and continued to help through the years. So these established mail-order millionaires still run small classified ads regularly. This does make a strong case for you to use classified ads. If small classified ads worked well for many mail-order millionaires, these ads should work for you.

MAIL-ORDER SUCCESS STORIES

Remember: The mail-order millionaires of today were once newcomers to mail order. They wondered how they might start and build a profitable mail-order company of their own. They thought about which items would be best to offer. They planned their classified ads and direct-mail offers carefully. They tested new ideas and found the right ones. And they kept on plugging. When one offer proved to be a dud, these operators didn't give up. They went back to the drawing board to find something else that would work. Let's take a look at some of these self-made millionaires of mail order.

John D. MacArthur saw opportunity in mail order. He became fabulously wealthy by parlaying a $2,500 mail-order insurance firm into a vast fortune. He was said to be worth $5 billion when he died in 1978.

The son of a Pennsylvania minister, MacArthur went to work for a Chicago insurance firm owned by his brother Alfred when he was 18. He later tried newspaper work but didn't care for it. After a stint with the Royal Canadian Flying Corps during World War I, he returned to the insurance business. With a loan of $2,500, MacArthur bought Bankers Life Insurance Company. This was at the time of the Great Depression, and it was difficult to get good quality salespeople. So he decided to try selling insurance by mail. This was the smartest move of MacArthur's career. His company prospered. Mail orders for insurance with Bankers Life came in continually. Before long, MacArthur was buying out other companies.

Here's something to remember about MacArthur. He kept his cool when he first started to make money: "I didn't want to change my lifestyle because I was afraid something might happen. I was on thin ice for the first 15 years." Many newcomers to mail order fold up their companies after their first year of business because of low profits. This attitude shows a lack of purpose and planning. Some companies do make a lot of money the first year. Others don't. The point is that many fortunes in mail order were built over many years. And in most cases, the first several years were uncertain and difficult.

Another mail-order success story is that of E. Joseph Cossman. This ingenious man made his fortune largely from showing others how to build wealth. But Cossman had a profitable organization called the Future Millionaires Club and many other enterprises—all moneymakers. He is proof that you don't have to put all your eggs in one basket.

Cossman's key purpose now is "to help others realize the dream that I had come true for myself. The whole secret is in sales—the market of supply and demand. It's there for anyone with initiative and know-how who wants to get it."

MAKING YOUR FIRST MILLION

To many people making a million dollars seems impossible. But one of the first musts for becoming a millionaire is believing that it's possible to become a millionaire. So here are some rules to help you on your way to becoming a mail-order millionaire.

1. Devise a plan for your future. The character of Luke in the film *Cool Hand Luke* said that he never had a plan or knew what he was going to do next. Maybe that's why his life added up to nothing. If you have a plan, write it down. Add to it and rewrite it if necessary. Perfect and improve it as best you can. Study it often.

2. Be realistic. Realize that there are obstacles in your path to success. Decide how they can be overcome or removed.

3. Increase your self-discipline.

4. Don't join a large corporation. The odds are great that you'll get lost in the corporate shuffle. It often takes many years to move up to the top positions in big companies. Your chances are better with a younger and smaller company with growth potential.

5. Use your free time wisely. Many people have become millionaires by devoting most of their time to their careers. Many millionaires are strongly motivated people who turned a hobby into a profitable business. These people never get discouraged even though they often put in 75 to 100 hours a week.

6. Rely on yourself. Depending on others can be frustrating and a disaster at times. A good example of self-reliance is Irving Thalberg, the legendary Hollywood producer during the Golden Age of films. Thalberg ruled over Hollywood like a prince in the 1920s and 1930s. His long period of illness as a youth gave him time to think about his future. In making his plans for a business career, he devised his own rules that he would live by: "Never take any one man's opinion as final. Never think your

own opinion is unassailable. Never expect help from anyone but yourself."

7. Think positively about your work, the future, and life itself. There really is power in positive thinking.

8. Do it now. This was the success formula of W. Clement Stone, Chicago insurance tycoon and multimillionaire. It helped him to build his own enormously successful business—Combined Insurance Company. Success does not come to one who waits. Always have a list of things to get done for every day. After you get the big things accomplished, you can then turn your attention to the less important ones. This is one of the most effective ways to get more done. Many top executives practice it consistently.

9. Develop your imagination. Imagination is a priceless creative ability. Walt Disney, Grandma Moses, Cole Porter, and Will Rogers became successful through imagination. Imagination can be especially helpful in mail order. Try to imagine what new inventions, services, and scientific advancements the future will bring.

10. Advertising is a growth industry. And as an operator of your own mail-order firm, you're part of this $117 billion-plus industry. Advertising will be a boom industry for the rest of this century and beyond. So learning how to advertise your mail-order products and services is worthwhile. There's a growing need for more informative, interesting, and effective advertising.

11. Trying something new can be the way to a fortune. It takes faith in yourself, but the payoff can be fabulous. Walt Disney's dream of an amusement park for children, built around his cartoon and film characters, eventually became Disneyland and Walt Disney World. How about the McDonald's fast-food success story? It was all started by Ray Kroc, a man who believed in a new idea.

    Many editors told DeWitt Wallace in the early 1920s that his idea for a magazine that would publish condensed versions of major articles was unworkable. But Wallace knew it would work. His idea became a reality in the form of the *Reader's Digest*.

12. Your customer list is another source of income for your mail-

order business. You can rent your list to other mail-order dealers, insurance firms, correspondence schools, publishers, and corporations. You can sell your list of names, but you'll only get one flat payment and nothing else. By renting your list, you will have a constant income source. A big list company like Dunhill can offer your list to literally thousands of businesses. So when you get enough customers to make it worthwhile, you can increase your income by renting your name list to professional list firms.

FACTS FOR YOUR MAIL-ORDER FUTURE

Here are some facts about Americans—compiled by the Census Bureau—that can be useful in planning your future in mail order:

1. Life expectancy is increasing. A girl born today is expected to live to her late 70s.
2. Nine out of 10 people are satisfied with their family life. But three out of 10 want divorce made easier to obtain.
3. The divorce rate is not as high as in recent years, but it has more than doubled since the 1950s. There are now three times as many children associated with divorce as there were 20 years ago.
4. The most popular type of outdoor entertainment is horse racing. It presently draws over 60 million fans—about double the number of fans who watch baseball, which is in second place. Greyhound racing comes in third, with professional football and basketball in fourth and fifth positions.
5. Television is the favorite pastime of three out of 10 people.
6. Americans are better educated now than at any other previous time in history. But they lack practical knowledge. Twenty percent of adults are functional illiterates.
7. The crime rate is skyrocketing. Crimes against people and property have tripled in less than 20 years.
8. The average family size is declining.

Remember: You may never become a millionaire by running a mail-order company, but the opportunity always exists. Having your own business and seeing it continue to prosper year after year is always exciting. And the chance to one day hit the mail-order jackpot is a continuous challenge.

22

Data-Base Marketing in the 1990s and Beyond

One of the clear signs of the new age we're living in is the bright new spotlight on data-base marketing. Many shy away from getting started with it, but they're missing an opportunity. Habits are difficult to break, and the business-as-usual philosophy can hold you back.

High technology is in the center arena these days. Keeping an open mind about the possibilities that today's technology makes possible is an important basic in making a start with data-base marketing and using it to build your mail-order business.

Thomas Lewis, former information executive for both the White House and American Express and now president of Technology Management Group, has summed up the information explosion well: "The volume of information that firms have to handle requires a much higher level of information technology than five years ago."

WHAT IS DATA-BASE MARKETING?

Marketing writer and authority Richard Cross defines data-base marketing as "simply using information about buyers and prospects to interact with them."

Perhaps the most rapid growth has taken place in mail-order, data processing oriented business supplies. More automation has come, there is smarter use of telemarketing, fulfillment, and customer service, and the setting up of geographic distribution centers is achieving fast delivery.

In the business supplies industry, chains of discount office product retailers are bringing more price competition. Many retail chains offering lower prices are moving into the mail-order market.

Before you can employ data-base marketing techniques in your mail order business, you must:

1. Determine what your specific marketing goals are.
2. Collect the data you need to reach your goals.

SOME ADVANTAGES OF THE DATA-BASE

There are several reasons for using a data-base, including the following:

- A data-base provides an abundance of information to study and analyze.
- It lets you discover which market group uses your product, how they use it, and when.
- It helps you stay ahead of your competition.
- It indicates who your customers are, and if they're likely to buy the same type of product again.
- It helps to determine if a new product is likely to work.
- It is a good way to assume a larger share of the market.

What all this means is that you will sell more of your product and offer items by using a data-base, once you have one in place.

WHAT IS USED TO BUILD DATA-BASES?

The buying practices of customers are being tracked daily by a number of big companies. Most of the time when consumers ask for a discount, enter a sweepstakes, or order merchandise by mail or telephone, their names, addresses, and what they bought all goes into ever-expanding company data-bases.

Big corporations like Hallmark Cards and Proctor and Gamble use direct mail, general advertising, and telephone programs to collect data on prospective customers. Pepsi-Cola uses a summer promotion with a discount card offered to kids to develop their mailing list. Kimberly-Clark purchases name lists of new mothers and then sends brochures, coupons, and new product information. This material is sent during the diaper-wearing stage of babies. Proctor and Gamble collects data via reply cards sent to customers offering free product samples by mail.

HOW LONG DOES IT TAKE?

Most experts agree that it takes from two to four years to build a dependable, reliable data-base.

Data-bases can tell you a lot about your customers. But sometimes they lead to a dead end. According to Alan Gottesman, a Paine-Webber analyst, "If it costs $1.35 to get someone to try a 75¢ product and there's only a 30 percent chance he's going to buy it again, forget it." For this reason some companies only send coupons through the mail.

Kraft has joined the data-base bandwagon. Kraft Foods has established a data-base of 20 to 25 million users of its 140 food products. The lists compiled are of likely product users. John Kuendig, Kraft's present direct-marketing chief (for General Goods USA), says it this way: "When we mail to someone's house, our ability to communicate with them and give them a message is much stronger than any other medium."

L. L. Bean, a mail-order company for outdoorsmen that takes special pride in its service, promises "100 percent satisfaction or your money back." Through analysis of their data-base, the Bean Company has discovered that customers are becoming more demanding, given the competition between mail-order merchants and retailers."

What seems to be happening is that each segment of business is developing its own program of data-base marketing. Business supplies, retail, newspapers, soft drink companies, travel bureaus, and direct sales companies have all started their own data-bases.

As you build your mail-order business you can insure continued growth by developing your own data-base. Here are some suggestions for getting your data-base started:

- Send a questionnaire (asking key questions) to those who buy from you at least once.
- Use coupons your customers can return to get free product samples as an incentive.
- Group categories of products or services and ask customers to check those categories that include items they would consider buying.

- Ask your customers for opinions and suggestions.
- Send your customers a "What I Liked About the Product" sheet for them to complete and return.
- Call a certain percentage of your customers and ask them key questions concerning your offerings. This can save you time, but it's usually better to have customer reactions on paper too.

Track all of this information in your data-base, and you'll find that your business will be able to determine how best to satisfy your customers, resulting in better profits.

For your own mail-order growth, I've heard a number of good reports about the Quiken Software. It's reportedly great for mail-order businesses, keeping up with customer names and addresses, who bought what, prices, and other records and information you need to have on hand. And Quiken Software is user friendly.

Take your lead from the big companies. As your mail-order business grows, develop your own data-base—keeping control over the costs involved. There's no question that once in place your own data-base can increase the number of orders you receive, and, subsequently, your profits.

23

The Sure Way
to Mail-Order Profits

Mail order is interesting, challenging, and rewarding. It's very satisfying to create a brand new product or service of your own, advertise it, and then build it into a consistent winner.

John D. Rockefeller once offered some excellent advice: "When you hear about a good thing, don't delay. Get in while you can." Mail order is a good thing. And you should do well in it. But there are pitfalls to avoid, and you'll soon find that mail order is a business in which common sense can pay off in cold, hard cash.

MAIL ORDER IS A BUSINESS OF IDEAS

Remember: Mail order is a business of ideas. You need ideas for products and services. You need ideas to advertise these offers. I want you to recall three dynamic ideas. Each one has earned a fortune. The paper clip is the first. It's been around for a long time and is always useful—but think about how simple it is. The second idea is the game of Monopoly. It's still the best-selling game ever made. Think of the pleasure it has brought to people everywhere. Think of how Monopoly offers each player a chance to be a rich property owner for a while—even though it's only a game. Think of the wide appeal it has. The third idea is the hula hoop. It may have been a fad, but it made its originator wealthy. It caught the imagination of the public and sold like mad. The public—young and old alike—

just couldn't resist buying the hula hoop and trying it out. It was a real winner.

Now here's the point: Blockbuster ideas can make you rich. Sometimes all you need is one good idea. And you have just as much chance as anyone else to come up with a great idea for a mail-order product.

MAIL ORDER IS A BUSINESS OF PRODUCTS

Start thinking now about products. Saturate your mind with old products, new products, any products. Time spent thinking about them is not wasted. Look at mail-order publications of 20 or 30 years ago. What was selling well then? Sometimes bringing back an old product is highly profitable. You never know when a new product idea will come to mind. It could develop into a blockbuster and make a fortune.

Here are some important characteristics to consider when you have a mail-order product in mind. Use the following list as a guide when you compare your product to competing ones.

1. Price
2. Size and weight
3. Versatility
4. Appearance and style
5. Performance
6. Durability
7. Accuracy or speed
8. Convenience
9. Installation cost

YOUR PROJECTED SALES VOLUME

There's power in expectation. So you should set sales volume goals for your mail-order business. When you start your company, ask yourself what your sales volume should be for your first six months or year in business. Here is a good way to record these sales goals:

First Year	First Product	Second Product	Total Sales
	$ _____	$ _____	$ _____
Units	_____	_____	_____
Second Year	$ _____	$ _____	$ _____
Units	_____	_____	_____

The following Small Business Administration booklets may be of help to you. They can be obtained from the Superintendent of Documents, Washington, D.C. 20402. At this time of writing, the booklets are free. Here are the titles:

- "What Is the Best Selling Price?" MA No. 193.
- "Marketing Planning Guidelines" MA No. 194.
- "Are Your Products and Channels Producing Sales?" MA No. 203.
- "Keep Pointed Toward Profit" MA No. 206.
- "Marketing Research Procedures" SBB9.
- "National Directories for Use in Marketing" SBB13.

THE ROAD TO MAIL-ORDER SUCCESS

As you proceed along the road to mail-order profits, the following guidelines will help you. They will increase your profits, develop your confidence, and keep you moving ahead. Most of them have made a great difference in my own life. They can do the same for you. When used with the right mail-order products, these guidelines can lead you to substantial success.

1. Study—Continue to learn all you can about mail order. There's always more to learn about this interesting and challenging industry.
2. Choose Your Offer Carefully—Again, much of the success of your business will depend on the quality of your products or services. Choose them carefully. When one flops, try something

else. Don't get discouraged if your first items do poorly. Thomas Edison tried 10,000 times before finding the right filament for the electric light.

3. Use Effective Advertising—Copy is king. Your job is to use the most effective form of advertising (classified ad, display ad, direct mail, or catalog) and to select the best copy. Choosing the best mail-order publications for your ads is also important.

4. Find Your Proper Rate of Growth—This will be determined by your own goals. Try to set a realistic objective for your first year in the business. You may decide to reach a certain level of growth and then remain at that point. It's up to you. But remember: Smaller goals, once realized, build confidence for achieving bigger goals. And real success doesn't come overnight.

5. Develop the Will to Win—Your own will, once aroused, developed, and well focused on your goals, is a powerful force. Margaret Mitchell, author of *Gone With the Wind,* spent 10 years of her life writing her novel. She said little about her work while creating it and was frequently kidded by friends for giving so much of her time to writing. But Margaret Mitchell knew what she wanted and she went ahead and wrote a successful novel. She was enormously talented, but talent alone—without willpower—isn't enough. Most great achievements have resulted from a strong combination of both. You have the potential to attain real success in mail order: "Whatever the mind of man can conceive of can become a reality." Talent, ability, and knowledge are all important, but the human will can work wonders.

6. Use Your Imagination—This is real magic. Use your imagination to think of one good product idea and it could make you rich. Set your first-year goals and use your imagination to reach them. And remember: Enthusiasm fires the imagination.

ASK WHAT YOU CAN SELL FOR PROFIT

Finding what you can sell for a profit is one of the most vitally important things you will do before launching your business.

Thomas Edison learned an important lesson as a young man. He came up with his first patented invention, an automatic vote recorder designed to speed up the vote tally in legislative bodies. Unfortunately, his invention bombed. But Edison never forgot the lesson. He often said the following: "Anything that won't sell, I don't want to invent." You should follow the same guideline. If it won't sell by mail order for a reasonable to good profit, forget it.

In the words of New York consulting executive Marc Particelli: "Most big American companies now are systematically scanning the world for new product ideas." American concerns are virtually copying consumer goods from such distant places as Tokyo and Paris and presenting them here in the States as new products.

But what works well overseas might not do as well here in the States. Above all, you need to offer a product or service you personally believe in and can sell with pride and professionalism. Even if your first offer proves to be a dud, it can be an important lesson for you. You will have gained some experience, knowledge, and the feeling of what it's like to be in business for yourself. The next item you offer could well be a different story.

THE COST OF A PART-TIME MAIL-ORDER BUSINESS

How much will it cost you to launch a mail-order company as a sideline? It depends on the product or service being sold. Many mail-order firms have been launched with as little as a few hundred dollars. But with today's rising prices, you would need $500 to $1,000 at least. You need letterheads and envelopes, record books to keep track of the orders you receive, and other similar supplies. A word processor or good typewriter is a must, since all of your business letters should be typed neatly on your letterheads.

Don't forget to figure in the cost of your first test ads. If your ad pulls enough orders, you'll want to run it in other leading mail-order publications. All these are essential expenses that you must add up to get a close estimate of your total expenses.

GIVE YOUR PART-TIME BUSINESS ENOUGH TIME

If you intend your business to be a sideline venture, you should still try to put a few hours or more into it every day. Once you have everything in place, it may not take long to keep it running smoothly. Set aside time for writing ad copy, thinking of possible product-service items, filling orders, and running your business.

Hold conferences with yourself. Decide where you would like to be with your mail-order business in five or 10 years. Determine the goals you want to achieve with your business, and try to write out the specific steps you can take to accomplish them.

Keep in mind at all times that there's no limit on how far you can go in the business. The right products and services, well advertised, can turn your venture into a real success story.

THE BEST SEASON FOR MAIL ORDER

Mail order thrives during the autumn season. Many rate it as the best time of the year to be advertising. January is also very good, but February can fall off a bit; October is often as good as, or even better than, September.

One basic reason for the strong fall season is that autumn marks the end of the summer doldrums. The business world perks up when fall sets in. The mail-order industry comes alive with fresh plans, new ideas and products, and potential. There's a spirit in the air that almost grabs prospects and urges them to respond to ads. Most vacations are over when fall arrives, and there's a return to the regular routine of doing business.

The response you get from a given ad in a magazine depends on the month of circulation. In summer, people are outside and don't read ads as much as they do in cooler months. There's not much mail-order action in December either. People are afraid to order by mail in this month, fearing that they won't get their gifts in time for Christmas. The big mail-order months begin with September and January. But many mail-order companies run ads all year round, perhaps cutting back a bit in late spring and summer. Of course, your choice will vary depending on the type of product you plan to sell. Seasonal items such as Christmas ornaments will sell well only before and during the Christmas season.

The larger mail-order companies will often run ads in the poor months to test new products. But they have the money to do so. If results are good, they will estimate the percentage increase when the ad is repeated in a better month.

If you have little money to spend, you'll want to stack the cards in your favor. You should try to make your first ads pay out by running only in the best pulling months. Let's say you run your first ad in May, and it pulls 230 orders. How many orders can you expect the same ad to pull in October? Generally, October should pull about 40 percent more orders than May. You therefore multiply 230 orders by 1.40 and get 322 orders. That's what you can expect to get in October.

Some advice for a beginner in the business is to advertise only in the good mail-order months (September through November, and January through March). You could stay out of low pulling months. Remember, too, that certain products lend themselves more to specific times of the year than others.

To get all the orders you can during the busy fall season, put your creative imagination and copywriting skills to good use. Devise powerful advertising that compels customers to buy. Having an attractive product or service to offer is very important to your success, but actually landing the sale is most crucial.

Unless you motivate your prospects to take action and send you an order without delay, your offers won't move. You need a steady flow of orders coming in to keep your business growing, whatever the season. The ability of your ad to close sales will determine your degree of success.

Unlike those who sell to prospects on a face-to-face basis, in mail order you depend on the total effect and pulling power of your ads. You don't have the prospective buyer sitting beside you, or across a table, so you have no chance to address objections or answer questions about the offer. Your prospect cannot try out the product on the spot. The words of your classified ad or direct mail sales letter represent you and your offer; they must answer all objections and questions. The overall sales appeal must be strong enough to make your prospect decide to send you an order.

Remember the statement of Claude Hopkins, one of the most brilliant advertisers of this century: "The only purpose of advertising is to make sales." Ad writers sometimes forget they are salespeople and try to be performers. Instead of sales, they seek applause. Don't try to be amusing unless that will increase your profits.

A certain flair for the English language will reduce the risk in running your business. If you only plan to sell a few basic products, this obviously won't be all-important. But the more products you sell via mail order, the more copywriting you will be planning and writing. In the latter case, a deep love for working with words will prove invaluable to you.

On the other hand, if you don't feel confident about working with words, don't let it keep you out of mail order. You can learn how to use words effectively. Ad writing is a craft, and a craft can be learned.

A PROVEN GUIDE FOR SUCCESS

Known as "The father of modern publicity methods and practices," Phineas Taylor Barnum believed in and followed a highly moral code of showmanship. His proven guide for success is still valid today and can increase your chances for success in mail order.

High on Barnum's list of steps for success is this practical pointer: "Select the vocation which is most congenial to your tastes." Millions of people dislike the work they do each day because they made the wrong vocational choice. Take stock of your own situation. Life goes by fast, so you should be doing the kind of work you like.

Let Money Work for You

"Let money work for you" is another Barnum suggestion. A growing savings account is money at work for you. "Every man needs a nest egg—a cash reserve," said Bernard Baruch, the great Wall Street financier. When an opportunity comes along, a cash reserve will enable you to take advantage of it.

Putting money to work can also mean investing it in a mail-order company of your own. Investing has paid off for a lot of people. Although Bob Hope, Steve Allen, and Gene Autry have earned a lot of money from their careers, a large part of their fortunes were built through wise investments. The money you put into your mail-order company could turn out to be the best investment of your life.

Beware of the Horror of the Blues

Another tip on Barnum's guide for wealth and success is "not to let the horror of the blues take over you." Fight the blues with all your might, for they can wreck your plans and wipe out your enthusiasm. There's a definite way to send the blues packing every time. When a negative thought tries to take root in your mind, just pull it out. Allow only positive and constructive thoughts of success. Weed out the others. It takes a lot of mental discipline to keep negative thoughts out of your mind, but it's worth the effort.

Whatever You Do, Do It with All Your Might

"Whatever you do, do it with all your might" is the next Barnum pointer for success. If necessary, work at your goals day and night. Put your entire self into your projects, calling on all your powers to help you accomplish your aims. Be determined. There's tremendous power in a determined person, power that won't take no for an answer. If a profitable and successful mail-order business is what you want, get it! Don't give up on your goal. Make what you want a reality.

Ask yourself some key questions. Where would America be today if it had given up in 1776? What would the fate of the Union have been if Lincoln had given up his determination to preserve it? What would have happened to England if it had not taken a stand against Hitler? Remember: With determination, anything is possible.

Learn Something Useful

Barnum also believed in learning. "Learn something useful to fall back on" is one four-star ingredient in his recipe for success. Have an alternate plan in case your original one doesn't work. Barnum himself is a good example. He had worked as a grocery store clerk after leaving grammar school, so the first thing he did after moving to New York in 1834 was to open a grocery store. Eight years later, Barnum opened the American Museum. He had natural ability as a promoter, but he had his grocery business to fall back on if necessary. Your knowledge of mail order could prove to be the "something useful" you have to fall back on.

Another example is Thomas Jefferson. He had a great desire to learn something useful every day of his life. He spent five years preparing himself for law, but he didn't limit his study to that field alone. So beside law, Jefferson studied political science, philosophy, Spanish, Italian, German, and some American Indian languages. Through the years, he learned many useful things that helped him to become a lawyer, statesman, scientist, architect, farmer, inventor, and musician. If Jefferson's career as a lawyer had ever floundered, he could fall back on the other skills he had learned.

Depend on Your Own Personal Exertions

"Exercising both caution and boldness, depend on your personal exertions," advised Barnum. At 19, Barnum founded and edited a newspaper in Danbury, Connecticut. Most worthy accomplishments and achievements depend on personal exertions. Students who earn academic degrees learn this early. They know they have to keep plugging away at the books to get their degrees. One college professor, in summing up the trials and tribulations of getting a Ph.D., said it was like jumping through flaming hoops. He just kept jumping through them until he got his degree. Your own effort can pay off in many ways.

Be Systematic

Another of Barnum's directions is "to be systematic and to have the time and place for everything." Even the Bible backs this up and states that "there is a time for everything—a time to live, a time to work, a time to die." To keep advancing toward the success you seek, list each night—in order of their importance—the things you must do the next day. Then do these things. Planning your work and working your plan is a system that always works if you stick to it.

Advertise Your Business

This is, of course, essential for someone entering the mail-order field. Barnum felt that "advertising your business is a must." If you don't sing the praises of your business, who will?

When Barnum realized that his own name was a big factor in his success, he fully exploited it. He's been compared to Shakespeare for his advertising genius and eloquence. When word spread that P. T. Barnum would be present for a circus performance, the box office take was always higher. Many people were just as interested in seeing the prince of showmen as his circus. But remember: Although Barnum was the author of statements like "there's a sucker born every minute," he drew a sharp line between innocent humbug and fraud.

Read the Newspapers

A final must for success, according to Barnum, is to "read the newspapers." Barnum evidently learned that the New York museum was for sale by reading a newspaper. Opening his American Museum was an important step in his career. "All I know is what I read in the papers," said Will Rogers. Ideas that have led many to success and riches have come from reading newspapers regularly.

Barnum's System Works

Phineas T. Barnum followed his own rules, including one he listed as "preserving your integrity." He liked his notoriety, but he always gave the public more than it paid for, and he made sure that his shows were in good taste. He firmly believed that the public deserved wholesome amusement.

P. T. Barnum practiced what he thought daily and was widely known and loved for his sunny, alive nature, his constant desire to make people happy, and the improvement he brought to every town in which he lived. In the eyes of the public, he was a living Horatio Alger hero. When he died in 1891, his last words were a request to know the circus receipts for the day. Barnum was worth $5 million when he died. That was quite a fortune for that time. He was rich not only in money, but also in friends, family, and a sense of accomplishment.

As you plan your future in mail order, keep Barnum in mind. His ideas are well worth following today. Mail order is advertising and promotion. And P. T. Barnum was a brilliant promoter and advertising genius. Barnum's guide to success has helped me to make money in mail order and to become a widely published writer, copywriter, songwriter, college teacher, public speaker, winner of national awards, and advertising consultant. So refer to his words of wisdom often and try to apply his proven guide for success in your own life and mail-order business.

The Magic of a Fresh Start

Nothing helps a person more in life than making a fresh start. You may have tried to find your place in other industries without much success. If so, then a mail-order business of your own could be just the fresh start you need. Perhaps launching a mail-order company will be your first experience in the world of business. Whatever your situation may be, the freshness and stimulation of a new start can work wonders in your life. But for every person who dares to make a fresh start, millions of people are afraid to take the plunge and don't realize that what they need in their lives is new enthusiasm. A mail-order business can provide this enthusiasm.

WELCOME TO THE WORLD OF MAIL ORDER

Use this book when making your start and refer to it often. I know that you can be a part of the exciting future of mail order. Whether you stick with a few products or grow into a giant business, a lot of satisfaction and personal fulfillment await you in this industry. Maybe one of your products or services will improve the lives of your customers. It's a nice feeling to know that you've made a contribution to others and to the world in which you live. Bernard Baruch said it well: "The future is actually bright with promise. The trend of civilization itself is always upward." Welcome to the mail-order business. May your products be consistent winners, your ads pull stacks of orders, and your profits make all your dreams come true.

Appendix 1

Checklist for Success in Mail Order

1. Remember that mail order is an item business.
2. Use short, attractive headlines to hook prospects into reading your classified ads.
3. Try to acknowledge every order you receive. It's good business.
4. Consider offering a self-improvement booklet—their sales have skyrocketed.
5. Be sure to use a professional-looking letterhead for all of your business correspondence. And type your letters.
6. Avoid pie-in-the-sky copy in your ads offering unbelievable promises or overnight riches. Don't try to fool prospects. Offer genuine value for their money.
7. Watch for important trends in the industry.
8. Look over the "Window Shopping" mail order section of *House Beautiful* every month.
9. Develop your creative abilities.
10. Think about products or services you could offer to moonlighters. There are currently about five million people in the United States holding down two jobs.
11. Sell low-priced items directly from an ad for best results.
12. Guarantee your products and offers. You'll get more orders.
13. Avoid any offer that smacks of a chain letter or pyramid scheme.
14. Set a regular time for thinking up new product and service ideas for your business.

15. Offer a short manual on any subject—they often sell well.

16. Keep track of your growing customer list. An index card system is a good method.

17. Clip out classified and display ads that you feel are especially effective. Save them for future reference.

18. Consider offering a product to help people lose weight. There's a huge worldwide market for this type of item.

19. Allow for the rising postage rate in your direct mailings.

20. Make use of the "you appeal" in your ads.

21. Think of a way to prevent computers from being manipulated. Computer embezzlement is increasing weekly. Corporations will pay well for a computer theft prevention product or service.

22. Use inquiry and follow-up classified ads for higher-priced offers.

23. Always think ahead.

24. Don't use a catalog to sell your offers until your customer list has at least 10,000 names.

25. Remember the dominant wants of people. Try to offer items that include many of them.

26. Always enclose a reply envelope—preferably a postpaid one.

27. Know that $100.00 spent on a direct mailing to 1,000 names should return you $300.00 or more. Anything less is not profitable enough. Rising postage rates will call for adjustment of these figures in the years ahead.

28. Before you offer a new product or service, decide who your customers are, and the best form of advertising to reach them with.

29. Know that you're bound to find a winner sooner or later.

30. Keep new ideas developing in the back of your mind. The safety razor with its removable blade made its originator a millionaire.

31. Be sure to appeal for action by asking prospects to send you an order.

32. Offer some kind of a pet product by mail.

33. Use headlines printed in black and red on the outside envelope (the envelope received by prospects).

34. Keep your eyes and ears open for profitable new business ideas.

35. Handle any complaints immediately. Respond with a courteous letter of explanation.

36. Think about what kind of information, instruction, or special sounds you could put on record or tape and sell by mail. Cassette sales are exploding.

37. Use the extra incentive of a free bonus gift. It's a proven way to increase your orders.

38. Try new selling strategies. Experiment by changing the headlines, copy, and size of your ads.

39. Use a short, easy-to-remember name for your mail-order company.

40. Advertise consistently—it's the best way to make money in mail order.

41. Offer a product that cannot be bought in retail stores.

42. Be sure to use a P.S. at the end of your direct-mail sales letter. It gives your offer extra pulling power.

43. A street address inspires more trust that a post office box. The rental fee is small.

44. Know that more and more married women are working full-time outside of the home.

45. Realize that a person's richest accomplishments may take place after the age of 20.

46. Work first with manufacturers in your own area or nearby when you use a drop-ship arrangement.

47. Remember that the names you receive from requests for details on your offers can grow into a profitable mailing list.

48. Offer a correspondence course. Many of the home-study firms in the United States are operated by individuals.

49. Write the copy for your ads with the mass audience in mind.

50. Look for items that serve the people of today. Smart mail-order operators change with the times.

51. Watch the ads in leading mail-order publications. Request details yourself, so you can look over current offers and literature used to sell them.

52. Don't start a mail-order company if you expect to make a fortune overnight.

53. Try to get the quality of sincerity into your sales letters. According to Billy Graham, considered one of this century's most effective communicators, "Sincerity is the biggest part of selling anything."

54. Realize that some of the big success stories in mail order have resulted from seeing a consumer need and then filling it.

55. Continually develop your imagination.

56. Subscribe to the *Gift and Decorative Accessories Buyer* magazine. It covers new items in the gift trade.

57. Start your mail-order business with small classified ads.

58. Sign all your outgoing letters. It creates a much better impression.

59. Don't let your age discourage you. Ray Kroc, the man behind the McDonald's restaurant success, didn't launch his McDonald's career until his middle 30s. He was past 40 before he became rich.

60. Write crisp, fresh copy for your ads. Make every word pull its weight.

61. Stick with a pulling ad until the returns from it begin to fizzle out.

62. Keep alert for items that will trigger repeat orders.

63. An order form built into your sales letter can save money, but a separate order form will usually pull more orders.

64. Hold frequent brainstorming sessions. Try to come up with new product and advertising ideas that will make your business grow.

65. Learn how to type. It can be a great help in your business.

66. Key every ad that you run so you can judge the pulling power of each publication and copy arrangement you use.

67. Practice writing sales letters until you feel confident that you can write a winner.

68. Keep a copy of every business letter you send out.

69. Know at all times what your competition is offering.

70. Avoid offering heavy items, so the shipping expense won't eat up your profits.

71. Visit gift centers in large cities and gift shows whenever possible. You'll find that these visits will stimulate new ideas.

72. Realize that "Five times as many people read a headline as read the body of an ad," according to David Ogilvy, a veteran advertising expert.

73. Know that the family of the future will be smaller, but more informed.

74. Offer a manual on solar energy and its use in heating homes. This should be a steady mail-order seller for years to come.

75. Delay launching a catalog until you've gained considerable experience and have enough items to make it worthwhile.

76. Send a refund at once to anyone who requests it.

77. Use color in your direct-mail package (sales letter, order form, circular, and reply envelope) whenever possible.

78. Keep your advertising copy simple.

79. Don't buy catalogs from existing companies with your own company name imprinted on them. You can do better offering your own items.

80. Realize that the great creators and thinkers of history stood alone against the people of their time. Practically all new ideas are opposed.

81. Open your ad with a powerful headline that grabs attention.

82. Be alert for new ideas constantly.

83. Realize that most checks received with mail orders will be good.

84. Try to offer a variety of items by mail. But do it slowly and carefully.

85. Keep close tabs on the amount of stock you have on hand for each item. Be sure you can fill all incoming orders, but avoid overstocking.

86. Realize that every great achievement came from the mind of some independent creator.

87. Treat all customers and prospects the way you'd like to be treated. The Golden Rule definitely applies to the mail-order business.

88. Try to select products and items that many people need.

89. Keep your customers informed about your new products or offers so they'll buy from you again and again.

90. Follow up on those who send you requests for details on an offer. If they don't send an order right away, try again later. Inquiry names have been sold on the 20th and 30th attempts, so don't be too quick to give up on them.

91. Quote your asking price for low-priced items in round dollars.

92. Use a broker with a reliable reputation whenever you rent a mailing list. Ask questions about the nature and quality of the list. There are all kinds of lists floating around. You should use the best ones.

93. Know that wealthy people show no special set of personality traits that make them different from ordinary people.

94. Be sure that every direct-mail package you send out includes a sales letter, order form, circular, and reply envelope.

95. Know that all mail-order publications are happy to send you free information on their current advertising rates.

96. Think about how William Lear originated the car radio, the Lear jet, the eight-track tape player, and over 150 other inventions. He often put in a 12-hour day—even at age 75.

97. Remember that the price range of products advertised in mail-order publications may vary widely.

98. Keep offering new items from time to time.

99. Do your best to fill all orders within 24 hours. This will help you build a list of satisfied customers.

100. Start out with a low-priced item, but try to sell a higher-priced offer as soon as you can, for it will be more profitable.

Appendix 2

Mail-Order Nuggets of Wisdom

In *The Uncommon Man in American Business,* Wallace Johnson highlights a significant point I urge you to keep in mind: "Too many people are thinking of security instead of opportunity. They seem more afraid of life than of death."

Big achievers keep their eyes on opportunity, which is a key factor to success. Keep in mind that some of the most wonderful ideas for new businesses, products, services, and inventions are yet to be originated.

TESTING

1. Test your ads with 2,000, 5,000, or more names from a list source.
2. Test in Sunday newspaper classified sections. This way you can find out quickly if the ad pulls. Magazines take months before the issue with your ad comes out.

It was Joe Karbo's superior, magnetic, full-page ad for his book, *The Lazy Man's Way to Riches,* that brought in many thousands of orders.

Before Karbo ran his ad, he spent considerable time and effort developing and perfecting it. He also *tested* it a number of times to be certain that he had a winner. When he first ran it as a full-pager, Karbo was very confident that his ad would do well. The profits proved to be far greater than his expectations.

ENTREPRENEURSHIP

Most people think of entrepreneurship as a person's desire and ability to run a business. An increasing number of colleges and universities are offering courses in entrepreneurship, and this trend will continue in the years ahead.

An undergraduate major in entrepreneurship has been established at Babson College in the greater Boston area. The new field lured 40 juniors when it first began. Babson College views an entrepreneur as "the originator or the principal mover of an enterprise. Such individuals are characterized by a willingness to take risks and to invest money and energy in the development of a service or product."

MAIL ORDER ON AN ADVANCED LEVEL

When you feel ready to move into mail order on an advanced level, I think that you will find my other mail-order book very helpful. *How to Make Money in Mail-Order* is a sequel to *Money in Your Mailbox* and approaches the subject of mail order on a more advanced level (paperback $14.95 and hardcover $29.95). The book may be obtained from the following address:

> John Wiley and Sons, Inc.
> Distribution Center
> Order Department
> 1 Wiley Drive
> Somerset, NJ 08875
> or by calling: (908) 469-4400

The book contains seven pages of mailing list companies, examples of sales letters that worked well, strategies for getting your product or service across, finding the money to build your business, dealing with competition, and much more. Above all, the book provides you with six key ways you can prosper in mail order.

The book also comes with extra resource materials to help you run your business on a daily basis. The discussion of mail order at the turn of the century will inspire you and make you even more glad you came into the field.

Appendix 3

Products Advertised in Typical Popular Catalogs

This list was gleaned from fall catalogs, so it naturally includes a number of Christmas items, but a wide variety of other products are also offered:

Family message centers

Porcelain knobs

Angel candle holders

Sewing kits

Soap crayons

Car lunch boxes

Anti-fog cloths

Mini lint brushes

Neck pillows

Cellular phones

Curio cabinets

Marriage plaques

Jogging suits

Nylon satin slippers

Home safes

Breakfast trays

Surprise boxes

Money magnets

Seven-piece decorating sets

Cameras

Rainbow paper clips

Brass seagull plaques

Colorful nail clippers

Snow pushers

Appendix 4

Where to Run Your Ads

The following magazines and publications are some of the leading places to run your ads. Because addresses change frequently, only the names are listed. Consult your library for up-to-date addresses.

Capper's (a weekly)
Entrepreneur
Entrepreneurial Woman (a new magazine)
Fate
Field & Stream
House Beautiful (Window Shopping section)
Income Opportunities
Income Plus
Modern Bride
Money
National Enquirer
New Business Opportunities
Opportunity Magazine
Outdoor Life
Popular Mechanics
Popular Science
Sports Afield
Spotlight
Star
Success
Wall Street Journal (mail-order section)
Winning
Workbench

Appendix 5

Helpful Resources

Here are some special resource publications I believe can be of help to you. Please bear in mind that the addresses given are subject to change at any time. They can be found in many libraries:

The Wholesale-by-Mail Catalog
Prudence McCullough, Editor
Harper Perennial
10 East 53rd Street
New York, NY 10022

The Directory of Mail-Order Catalogs Fourth Edition
Richard Gottlieb
Grey House Publishing
Pocket Knife Square
Lakeville, CN 06039

The Direct Marketing Mail Place
980 North Federal Highway, Suite 206
Boca Raton, FL 33432

Bibliography

Axtell, Roger E. *The Do's and Taboos of International Trade*. New York: John Wiley and Sons, 1991.

Bly, Robert. *Create the Perfect Sales Piece*. New York: Wiley Press, 1985.

Brabec, Barbara. *Homemade Money*. White Hall, Va.: Betterway Publishers, 1984.

Braun, Irwin. *Building a Successful Pro Practice with Advertising*. New York: AMACOM, 1981.

Burstiner, Irving. *Mail-Order Selling*. Englewood Cliffs, N.J.: Prentice-Hall, 1982.

Cohen, William A. *Building a Mail-Order Business*. New York: John Wiley and Sons, 1982.

Crown, Paul. *Building Your Mailing Lists*. New York: Oceana Publications, 1973.

Dennison, Dell. *The Advertising Handbook*. Bellingham, Wash.: Self-Counsel Press, 1991.

Edwards, Paul and Sarah. *Working from Home*. Los Angeles: Jeremy P. Tarcher, 1990.

Fox, Steven A. *Keys to Buying a Franchise*. Hauppauge, N.Y.: Barron's Educational Series, 1991.

Goldstein, Arnold S. *Starting on a Shoestring*. New York: John Wiley and Sons, 1984.

Hawken, Paul. *Growing a Business*. New York: Fireside, 1987.

Maul, Lyle, and Mayfield, Dianne. *The Entrepreneur's Road Map*. Alexandria, Va.: Saxtons River Publishers, 1990.

Ogilvy, David. *Ogilvy on Advertising*. New York: Crown Books, 1983.

Ringer, Robert. *Million Dollar Habits*. New York: Fawcett Crest, 1990.

Robinson, David. *What Is an Entrepreneur?* Holbrook, Mass.: Bob Adams, 1990.

Shilling, Dana. *Be Your Own Boss*. New York: William Morrow and Company, 1983.

Weiss, Kenneth. *Building an Import/Export Business*. New York: John Wiley and Sons, 1971.

Wilbur, L. Perry. *How to Make Money in Mail-Order*. New York: John Wiley and Sons, 1990.

Index